I0554715

BAD HENRY

The Murderous Rampage of
'The Taco Bell Strangler'

RON CHEPESIUK

WILDBLUE PRESS

WildBluePress.com

BAD HENRY published by:

WILDBLUE PRESS
P.O. Box 102440
Denver, Colorado 80250

Publisher Disclaimer: Any opinions, statements of fact or fiction, descriptions, dialogue, and citations found in this book were provided by the author and are solely those of the author. The publisher makes no claim as to their veracity or accuracy and assumes no liability for the content.

Copyright 2023 by Ron Chepesiuk

All rights reserved. No part of this book may be reproduced in any form or by any means without the prior written consent of the Publisher, excepting brief quotes used in reviews.

WILDBLUE PRESS is registered at the U.S. Patent and Trademark Offices.

ISBN 978-1-957288-70-3 Trade Paperback
ISBN 978-1-957288-71-0 eBook
ISBN 978-1-957288-69-7 Hardback

Cover design © 2023 WildBlue Press. All rights reserved. Interior Formatting and Cover Design by Elijah Toten www.totencreative.com

Praise for BAD HENRY
by Ron Chepesiuk

"Ron Chepesiuk [brings] the ghastly to life with deep research and brilliant storytelling. BAD HENRY uncovers new information and exposes deep-rooted challenges in the American criminal justice system."
—Bob Batchelor, award-winning
author of *Roadhouse Blues*

"[Here is a] well-researched, gut-wrenching story of a serial killer… true crime readers will not want to stop reading until the end."
—Barbara Casey, author of *Velvalee Dickinson*

"The hapless police never connect the dots until the always-in-sight coincidences point to the culprit. Ron Chepesiuk uses the serial killer's own words to set the stage for this engrossing true crime read."
—Alan Geik, author of *Uncle Charlie Killed Dutch Schultz*

"A gripping and gritty journey into the world of Bad Henry Wallace, a real-life serial killer who terrorized Charlotte, North Carolina for years before law enforcement connected his string of murders. Chepesiuk's research reveals eye-opening details into the creation and compulsions of society's most dangerous predator: one who kills for the thrill of it. Regardless of your stance on the death penalty, [Wallace} qualifies as a deserving candidate who admits to his crimes and taunts law enforcement with the possibility that more bodies could lurk in his history."
—Caroline Giammanco, author of *Inside the Death Fences and Bank Notes Revisited*

"Creative... captivating.... compelling!"
—Ron Fino, author of *The Triangle Exit*

"Readers are taken on a step-by-step dissection of the ten murders of African American women in the early nineties in east Charlotte, North Carolina. Like an adept medical examiner, Chepesiuk probes why Henry Louis Wallace did not fit the typical serial killer profile. With a city taken hostage for two years, doors and windows were shuttered while they awaited the next murder. Chepesiuk paints the painful story of charming fast-food restaurant manager, with links to each victim, who was overlooked for so long."
—David Larson, author of *The Last Jewish Gangster*

"True-crime master Ron Chepesiuk chronicles a nightmarish tale of an implacably evil killer as he outwits a police force slow to grasp the magnitude of what it's up against. The story has all the resonance of a horror movie, except that it happened in real life."
—Jerome Clark, author of *Hidden Realms*

BAD HENRY

*"There's the good Henry, and then there's the bad Henry.
As the years progressed, bad Henry took over."*
—Henry Louis Wallace, serial killer

CONTENTS

PROLOGUE

Murderous Rampage

On March 9, 1994, twenty-eight-year-old Henry Louis Wallace was feeling cocky. He had been on a murderous roll, rampaging in Charlotte, North Carolina, and the cops were clueless. Wallace had constantly watched the TV evening news for information that the police were on to him, but they still had not connected the dots. He smiled as he watched outraged Black citizens complain about the lack of action on the part of the police in solving the murders. They demanded to know: Was the lack of action because all seven victims were Black?

The Charlotte police conceded that they were stumped by the killings. And why should they not have been? After all, each case was being handled by a different police investigator. No notes were compared and no links made. The police treated each of the murders separately.

Wallace didn't fit the mold of a typical serial killer either. He looked normal. Around six feet in height, a little overweight, low key, disarming manner, Wallace could get lost in a crowd. He was slick, with a solicitous attitude, and women were taken in by his charm. He knew all of his victims and was able to gain the trust of each and every one of them. As author Anastasia Toufexis explained in a *Time Magazine* article, "(Women) invited him into their homes for dinner, watched while he cradles (sic) their babies in his arms, and accepted his invitations to date."

While Wallace was smug in his belief that he was gaming the system, he was also in desperate straits. His crack cocaine habit was out of control, and he didn't have the money for his next fix. He had learned that Vanessa Mack, a co-worker from Taco Bell, a popular fast-food restaurant, had received her income tax refund check from the IRS.

Mack was a petite, energetic young lady of 23 years, who seemed to always have a smile for anyone. Her dream was to be a nurse, but it was tough saving the money she needed to go to college. Still, she managed to salt some money away.

Wallace had seen Mack's ATM card, which she carried around with her. Surely, she would have some money in her bank account.

Wallace had totaled his green Maxima, so he caught a cab to Mack's apartment, hiding a pillowcase under his jacket. Mack would normally not let young men into her apartment, but this was Henry Wallace, Uncle Henry, harmless, someone who was trusted. He charmed Mack into letting him enter her apartment. In the kitchen, he snuck up behind Mack and wrapped the pillowcase around her neck. He squeezed hard and demanded she give him her ATM pin number.

Mack cried and struggled, but finally gave it to him. As she gasped, Mack pleaded with Wallace for her life, but he continued to squeeze the life out of her. Mack's limp body slumped to the floor. Wallace fumbled through her purse and found her ATM card.

Wallace dashed out of the apartment, caught a cab, and headed for Mack's bank, the Bank of America, where he tried using Mack's ATM card, but it didn't work. Mack had given Wallace a fake number.

Enraged, Wallace pounded the ATM. He was in a sweat, desperate for a fix. He thought for a moment, hailed a cab, and headed off into the night.

Wallace showed up at the apartment of his friend, Lamar "Squeaky" Woods, who he expected to be at work. Woods was a friend of Wallace and he and Wallace would hang out often in their free time.

Woods lived at the Lake Apartments in East Charlotte with his 18-year-old girlfriend, Brandi Henderson. She had worked with Woods and Wallace at the Golden Corral. Wallace planned to rob, rape, and murder Henderson.

Wallace rapped on the door of Wood's apartment and was surprised to see Woods answer. Brandi was at work, Woods told him. He was late for work, too, and had to leave.

Wallace turned around and walked away, anxious, frustrated. He still needed money for a fix. He remembered that he knew someone else who lived in the apartment complex—24-year-old Betty Baucom. Baucom knew that Wallace was the friend of the boyfriend of her girlfriend, Brandi Henderson, and she was more than happy to let Wallace use the phone.

When Baucom turned around to let Wallace into her apartment, Wallace grabbed and started to choke her. He demanded that she give him the alarm code and safe combination at the Bojangles where she worked as the assistant manager. Baucom resisted for nearly thirty minutes as Wallace got increasingly angry. Finally, Baucom surrendered the information and Wallace stopped choking her. He took the money from Baucom's purse but was disappointed at the amount. He then raped her. Afterward, Wallace told Baucom to get dressed and then strangled her to death.

The next day, Wallace brazenly returned to Baucom's apartment and took her VCR, checking to make sure she was still dead. Then he left Baucom's apartment and took her car, ditching it in a parking lot a few miles away. He wiped the steering wheel, seats, door handles, the interior, and most of the exterior clean of fingerprints.

Wallace caught a cab. Trekking back to his apartment, he was feeling smug about himself. He had got his drug fix while continuing to outsmart the police. The man who would become known as the Taco Bell Strangler had thought of everything. Or so he thought. The one thing he had forgotten: to wipe clean the finger and palm prints from Baucom's car trunk.

ONE

Bad Beginning

Henry Wallace would have few breaks in his early life. Many of the problems he faced later in life would stem from the problems and challenges he encountered in his childhood and teen years. Wallace's troubled youth surprised many in Barnwell who grew up with or came to know the amiable young boy who was always ready to listen or to give a helping hand when needed.

Ouida Swan Dest, who went to high school with Henry and served on the school's cheerleading squad, says she knew little about Wallace's impoverished background at the time of their association, but, today, wonders how Wallace could appear so upbeat and positive when he came to school with such a dysfunctional background. "He was just such a nice boy and so comfortable to be around," Dest recalled. "He was even allowed to pick up and drive the kids to school in the school bus. That's how much he was trusted."

Indeed, Wallace received a Certificate of Merit for "having operated a school bus for the 1982-83 year with an excellent record." After Wallace graduated from Barnwell High School, Principal W. Reed Swann wrote a character reference on his behalf regarding his conduct while at the school. Swann lauded Wallace for "never being involved in incidents of an aggressive or hostile nature, was well liked by his peers, and was supportive of the high school program."

Not all of Barnwell was impressed with Wallace, though. Aleah Thomas Cole of Barnwell dated Wallace from 1989 to 1990, and she recalled how he was a "gentle, generous and emotionally needy" boyfriend who lavished her with attention and gifts. But she came to see Wallace as being a "phony," elaborating, "He could adapt himself to any situation. It was just a farce because I had never seen a man who could cry at the drop of a dime."

Unfortunately, many women never saw past the charming façade, and they would pay for their lack of perception with their lives. Henry Louis Wallace was a chameleon in the worst possible way: a sadistic serial killer.

Henry Wallace was born dirt poor on November 4, 1965, in Barnwell, South Carolina. He had a sister, Yvonne, who was born on January 1, 1962, the fourth child and only girl to Lottie Wallace. Barnwell is a sleepy rural southern town located in the southwestern part of South Carolina about forty-two miles from Augusta, Georgia. The city has a population of nearly 5,000 people, more than half of them African American.

Wallace's mother, Lottie, who came to play such a seminal part in Henry's life, was born in 1946. Wallace's father walked out on Lottie, a heavy set, stern- looking woman, when she was pregnant. It was only one of many bitter disappointments Lottie encountered in dealing with the men in her life. It made her bitter, and she would often viciously take out her frustrations on her children.

Lottie was able to bond with her mother, but her mother died when Lottie was thirteen, a development that psychologists who studied the Wallace case say stymied her emotional development.

Lottie compensated for this loss by entering into an intimate relationship with a teacher who was married and at least 20 years older than her. The affair, which bore three children, lasted three years. While her lover provided for Lottie materially and emotionally, Lottie was to keep her mouth shut about their relationship, given the authority the male teacher had over her and the fact that he was much older. According to Carmeta Albarus, a certified social worker who later conducted a study of Wallace for his defense team at his trial, Lottie took out her anger from this relationship on son Henry. Albarus writes: "Throughout his entire life, Henry paid for the wrongs that had been done to his mother by the men in her life. She made him pay through a process of control, abuse, and intimidation. It started during the earliest stage of his development and continued through his adult years."

Lottie's lover never did provide material support for the children he had from Lottie. After Henry's birth, he ended the relationship and then quit his job and left town.

Young Henry lived in a dilapidated four-room shack with few necessities, including plumbing and electricity. His mother had to work long hours at the local textile mill struggling to make ends meet. The shack would remain his home until he was eighteen. The bathroom was nothing but a room with no running water and a set of chamber pots. Henry's daily chore was to empty out the chamber pots that contained the human waste. Henry shared a room with his sister and the waste pots remained in the room. Later, Wallace expressed one of his greatest fears while growing up: his school friends would see him emptying the chamber pots.

Henry never met his father and doesn't even know what he looks like. He lived with his mother, grandmother, and sister Yvonne, who was three years older. Yvonne maintained a protective, almost motherly attitude toward her brother. The mother and grandmother did not get along, however, and they fought constantly.

As the family's only means of support, Wallace's mother struggled to pay the bills and put food on the table.

The pressure of solely supporting the family was felt in how she treated her children. As criminologists Charisse Coston and Joseph Kuhns III explained in their study, *Lives Interrupted: A Case Study of Henry Wallace, an African American Serial Killer in a Rapidly Expanding Southern City,* "She demanded that her children grow up quickly."

To say Lottie Wallace was a strict disciplinarian would be an understatement. Lottie would make Henry hold his feces until he was forced to go in his pants. Then young Henry would be chastised severely for "messing in his pants." Terrorized by the thought of his mother finding out what he had done, Henry would often try to hide his soiled trousers or hurry home and wash his underpants before she could find out.

Lottie imposed strict rules on her children. She demanded that they get permission from her to take anything from the house. In punishing her children, Lottie often forced them to pick their own switch, which she would then use to whip them. Other times she would beat them with anything at hand, including a water hose, extension cords, and even tree limbs.

If she was tired from her day's work, she would get Henry and Yvonne to whip each other. Later in life, Henry would recall how painful it was for him to beat on his sister.

The abuse was not just physical, but also verbal. Lottie would constantly call Henry "stupid," "dumb," or a "son of a bitch," and complain that she wished she had never had him. He was ridiculed for his dark complexion, his mother joking that he had remained in the oven too long. He suspected that his sister was favored over him for her lighter complexion. Mother further degraded his girlfriends and routinely deprived Henry of his privacy by indiscriminately searching his room, wallet, and other belongings and, in adulthood, even his car.

He would never resist his mother's abuse, though, even when as punishment he was forced to walk around the neighborhood in his sister's clothing. Psychologists would later say that all these punitive actions warped young Henry's mind and created in him an inbred hatred of women. But it should be noted that other parents have been known to dress up their children in the clothes of the opposite sex, and those children didn't grow up to go out and kill members of the opposite sex.

As a kid, Wallace was deprived of many things, including toys. Once Henry's mother bought him a car set and then used the car tracks to beat him. When Henry tried to hide the car set, his mother found it and beat him.

Wallace developed a childhood fascination with the true detective magazines that his mother consumed. Wallace confided to FBI profiler Robert Ressler that he had "probably a collection of pornography magazines at that time that no kid my age would have. Probably few people older than me would have." Wallace estimated the number of magazines at fifty. He said he stole them from a convenience store and kept them stored under his bed.

Many of the stories in those detective magazines featured helpless victims, usually women, who were stalked and murdered. Many of the readers are normally adjusted fans of "who done it" literature, but psychologists and criminal profilers say they also attract serial killers. "He was certainly caught up in this kind of literature," explained Ressler. "He probably picked up a lot of ideas."

Wallace hung out on the tough streets of his blighted neighborhood. Crime was rampant, and Wallace had easy access to drugs, despite the tight control of his mother. According to Wallace, he started on heavy alcohol use at age 16 and then moved on to marijuana, LSD, and cocaine, which he usually smoked but used it once via IV. He claimed that he began hearing voices and "seeing a lady that I could touch," beginning about 1987.

When Henry was eight, he witnessed a high school girl being gang raped by a group of high school boys. Later,

Wallace recalled the incident: "Well, Victor and I was just messing around, and there was a whole bunch of older guys and there was Betty Jean. I'd say they were probably thirteen through sixteen and I remember Victor telling me, 'Come on, let's go.' It's like a little dirt road that led into the football field and had some woods on both sides. And then there was a school here. They took her into the woods, and we followed her, followed them into the woods, and it was like five or six guys. The only thing I remember her saying is 'wait', and she never said 'no', 'stop' or 'don't'. And I got turned on...."

Wallace had his first sexual experience at age four when he was molested by a seven-year-old girl from the neighborhood. The girl forced Wallace under a car, where she removed her skirt and panties and had him lay on her. Wallace claimed he didn't really know what he was doing, although instinctually he sensed it was something bad. The girl was caught and whipped, but Henry escaped physical punishment, although his mother laughed at him because she thought the girl was ugly.

Albarus' research found it did not help Henry that he was the only boy in the neighborhood at the time. Consequently, in the aftermath of this experience, Wallace would be molested by a string of young girls about seven to twelve years older than him over a ten-year period. A pattern developed whereby Henry would give a sandwich, juice, or flowers to a girl, and in return, he would be allowed to play with and kiss the girl's vagina.

Wallace grew up wondering about his father. He would frequently ask his mother about him, but she refused to reveal anything about him. One anecdote illustrates his tortured relationship with his father. It happened in teacher Mrs. Bennie Myers' first grade class at Barnwell Elementary School. Mrs. Myers asked her students, including Wallace, to tell something about their mom and dad. Henry had to admit he knew nothing about his father, not his name, what he looked like, where he worked. Nothing. The other kids in the class teased Henry. He cried.

Mrs. Myers came over to Henry and said, "Henry has a father, who is loving and good, a heavenly father. It is the same for everyone in the class."

In 1987, Wallace's mother ran into Mrs. Myers in Barnwell. The teacher remembered Henry and asked Lottie how he was doing. Later Lottie told Henry that she had seen Mrs. Myers and that she had asked about him. He went out and bought Mrs. Myers a Mother's Day card.

This is what Wallace wrote: "I know this is a big surprise to you, but I was equally surprised when my mom said you asked about me. I've been doing quite fine, and I hope you are as well. I also hope your Mother's Day is or was the best you've ever had."

Wallace would often fantasize about his father. Then one day the father called him on the phone out of the blue. He introduced himself and said he always wanted to meet him. Could that be arranged? Yes, of course, Henry responded excitedly. He wondered what his father looked like and how they would get along when they met.

One day, Wallace told all the kids in the neighborhood that he was going to finally meet his father. Henry played hooky from school and waited by the window in his house for his father to show up. Each car that turned the corner that day excited Henry, but soon turned to disappointment when the car kept going. But hope springs eternal. Henry waited that day, and the next, and the next. His father never did show up, and Henry was devastated. He never did get to meet his father.

The traumatic experience scarred Wallace for life. "That memory pained him by day and by night, in his busy hours and in his quiet hours," writes Coston and Kuhn in *Lives Interrupted.* "Life went on, but it dragged for some time after."

One of Wallace's mother's boyfriends served as a surrogate father. Parker, a man seventeen years older than Lottie and married, came into Henry's life when he was two years old. Parker treated Henry like a son, doing things with him like fishing and going to the ballpark. They became so tight that many in the community thought Parker was Henry's father. Henry even thought that Parker might be his father until Parker told Henry who his father really was.

One day, Parker decided to break off his relationship with Henry's mother. He had a conscience and told Lottie that she was a young woman and should not tie herself down with an older married man. He returned to serving his church, and Parker's relationship with young Henry ended.

According to Albarus' report, Henry "blamed his mother for the breakup between her and Parker. He recalled that Parker would call the house, but his mother would refuse his calls. He resented the fact that, after Parker, he had no male figure in his life."

In May 1996, Wallace underwent a neuropsychological evaluation that made this observation about him: "The patient reports that he was sexually molested by several girls, and he started molesting girls himself at the age of 15. He further reports a history of visual and olfactory hallucinations which began approximately at the age of 10 to (sic) 11. He reports that he often hears people laughing and giggling at him and female voices telling him to die. Wallace also claimed of 'seeing a lady that I could touch,' beginning in approximately 1987. He further reports mood swings in which he is 'hyperactive' for several days, which later develops to significant depression."

In a neuropsychological evaluation, Henry said that at age 10, he had been hit in the head with a bat and was briefly unconscious. According to the evaluation, Wallace reported possible olfactory hallucinations following this incident. The evaluation continued: "He had another incident at age 13 or 14 in which he was unconscious for several minutes from a skateboard accident, and claimed any 'cognitive deficits' from these accidents. Specifically, he had increased difficulties with mathematics and his attention span. He also reports that his ability to reason and logic diminished slightly following this accident, as well as his reading comprehension."

After participating in the Head Start Program, Wallace began first grade at the F. Myers Elementary School in Barnwell in 1972. He then attended Guinyard-Butler Middle School from August 1974 to June 1979 where Albarus notes: "Henry's performance, both academically and behavior wise needed improvement. There appeared to be significant decline in both areas. The pattern of not working up to his full potential was also evident by the records."

Wallace entered Barnwell High in August 1979 and graduated in December 1983. He did moderately well, but there is an indication that his academics suffered because of behavioral problems.

Wallace enjoyed high school. He was on his best behavior and teachers and students liked him. He became a member of the student council, the 4-H Club and the Vocational Center Student Council and worked as the newspaper staff photographer. Wallace received a letter of appreciation from Earle Morris, the South Carolina State Controller General, in which he was commended for his outstanding service to the community. In his lengthy letter, Morris said it was a pleasure meeting Wallace, and he noticed how popular Wallace was. Morris predicted, "I am confident that you will have a very successful future, Henry, if you stay on your present course."

His mother forbade him from joining the football team, so he became a cheerleader. The cheerleading squad was comprised of twelve to fifteen students, five of whom were Black. It was not automatic that one could join the cheerleading squad. One had to have an academic grade of C and a teacher's referral. Wallace made the grade. He was the only male on the roster, but that did not diminish his standing among his fellow students.

The female cheerleaders adored him. "Henry really fit in," Dest recalled. "I think everybody liked him."

Wallace was friendly and would often act as a kind big brother who would listen with a sympathetic ear and offer advice about boyfriend problems. He would make the women laugh. He was charming, upbeat, enthusiastic, and polite. He gave no hint of the man he would become.

Mrs. Janice Cave, a former Barnwell Elementary School teacher and sponsor of the cheerleading squad, recalled for Coston and Kuhn: "He got along well with all members of the squad. He was like a big brother to the girls." Mrs. Cave added that "he spearheaded the squad to do things that were only done at the college level."

Interestingly, despite the accolades, Wallace was arrested in May 1979 on a petty theft charge. He never went to court and was made to reimburse for the theft.

Even though Wallace was now in his teens, his mother continued her domineering role over his life. On his graduation night, he was forced to keep to a midnight curfew, even though his sister was allowed to stay up to 3 a.m. for the graduation. He feared the embarrassment of having his mother show up at the graduation to get him, but fortunately that did not happen.

Wallace's IQ was measured at ninety-two which is in the average range of functioning. He was 80th in a class of 126 at Barnwell High, and his grade point average was 2.09. His grades in college generally fluctuated from As in physical education to Cs, Ds, and Fs in algebra. His cumulative GPA at Denmark Technical College was 2.5.

When he graduated from high school in May 1983, he was not really excited about going to college, but he made an attempt. He wanted to attend Winthrop University in Rock Hill, South Carolina, but his ever-domineering mother forbade him to do so. He was forced to attend South

Carolina State College for a semester from August 1983 to December 1983, and Denmark Technical College for another ten months. Wallace put down on a U.S. Navy form that his major was nuclear engineering. Both schools were within commuting distance of his home, which allowed for his mother to check his car's odometer to ensure that he was only driving to and from school.

He was more interested in his evening job, working as a disc jockey off and on for about eighteen months at a small local radio station, WBAW. He emulated the famous disk jockey at the time, Wolfman Jack, and dubbed himself the "Night Rider." Listeners, especially the women, liked his voice and his easy-going manner. As a popular DJ, he had no problem getting dates. Later, Drew Wilder, station owner, recalled in a newspaper interview, "He was a pleasant sort of person. He had good manners, respectful." Wilder fired Wallace after he discovered compact discs were missing from the station.

Being a disk jockey might have ended up as being a career for Wallace, except for the fact that the good path he was following got derailed. In January 1988, he was caught breaking into a hardware store to find money to support his growing drug habit. He pled guilty to second degree burglary and was sentenced to two years of supervision. According to Patrick Seaburg, Wallace's probation officer, Wallace did not show up for most of his mandatory meetings.

Before this run-in with the law, Wallace took the path that many poor young Blacks pursued. He joined the United States Navy on December 12, 1984, for a four-year stint. He was assigned to the recruit training command in Orlando, Florida. He spent the next six years in the navy where he was stationed in Seattle, Washington; Pensacola, Florida; and New York City. He served on the USS Nimitz and the USS La Salle. Wallace did well, earning good reports for his service while traveling the world. Wallace advanced to an

E-4 level, but then went back to E-3 following a burglary and grand larceny charge.

Albarus reported that in one navy report, "Henry was described as an outstanding seaman who willingly followed all orders given to him and accomplished his assigned tasks in a timely manner. It was noted that his knowledge level was higher than expected of a seaman." He was also described as punctual, dependable, neat, and clean.

Wallace was promoted to third class petty officer before he left the service and qualified for a sea service ribbon. He was placed in charge of personnel senior to him. Wallace was discharged on August 30, 1989. His discharge papers noted that he had "served with honors."

But it seemed Wallace could not shake free of his mother's dominance even when it came to his earnings. Even after he joined the service, he would have to turn over a good part of his navy salary to his mother. Wallace directed that between $200 and $250 from his paycheck per month be sent to his mother. Wallace would complain, "I could not even buy my own things. I never owned a pair of designer sneakers until I was in the military."

In 1985, he married his high school sweetheart, Maretta Brabham, a quiet and submissive young woman whom he had dated off and on since his sophomore year at Barnwell High. It was a volatile relationship and the couple broke up several times. Prior to their marriage, Maretta had a child named Teondra by another man, but that did not seem to bother Wallace, who embraced the girl. He wanted a child of his own, but Maretta did not want to bear any more children. According to Wallace, his wife had been raped as a teenager, and this caused her to be frigid, which put an additional strain on their marriage. Wallace suggested they see a counselor, but she refused.

In May 1988, the navy informed Wallace that it had overpaid him $1200 and that there was no proof that Wallace had a dependent daughter. According to the navy, this made the payment unauthorized. In a letter to the navy, Maretta claimed that the $1200 was going to her husband's mother who had been kind enough to pay the bills for daughter Teondra's birth. And as for receipts, Maretta said that receipts had not been saved, given that "neither Henry or (sic) I knew a situation like this would arise…"

During one of Henry's and Maretta's separations, Henry met and hit it off with Henrietta Wiley, a barber. Henrietta would sit with Henry while he DJed. It was a good relationship, and Wallace even wanted to marry Henrietta, but his mother objected to the relationship, claiming Henrietta did not have a promising future.

On one occasion, when on leave from the navy, he went to visit Henrietta in Charleston, South Carolina, without telling his mother. Wallace was spotted by a cousin who told Henry's mother. Furious, Lottie went looking for him, calling every hotel in Charleston, but she could not find him. She eventually called the barber shop where Henrietta worked and got the number of Henrietta's sister. Lottie called the sister's number to find out the hotel where Henry was staying. Lottie read her son the riot act. Leave Henrietta and come home now, she ordered. Henry obeyed.

Nevertheless, wife and child joined Wallace as he transferred out to the West Coast. Still, Wallace could not stay out of trouble. He had become addicted to crack cocaine. To get the money to pay for his habit, he began breaking into businesses and homes to steal property that he could pawn. He was caught breaking and entering into a naval base. Given his good record, the navy gave him an honorable discharge. Wallace had slipped through the cracks. It would be a pattern to his life that would be repeated many times.

By now, however, his marriage was over, and with his dismissal from the navy, no one encouraged Wallace to seek counseling. Then his wife left him. Henry appeared willing to work their problems out, but she was not. Wallace separated from Brabham in 1992, but never divorced.

The marriage break-up was devastating to Wallace, and he became suicidal, attempting to kill himself by taking an overdose of pills. Wallace's life took a turn for the worse of increasing mental and psychological problems as he struggled to find adequate employment while his drug use increased. According to Albarus, "Family members who were interviewed maintain that it was after Henry's failed marriage that his problems began."

Wallace was fired from his job as chemical operator for Sandoz Chemical Company in Barnwell. Now with a growing drug habit, Wallace broke into the radio station where he had worked and stole video and recording equipment, but was caught trying to pawn them. With his life on a downhill spiral, Wallace decided a change in scene was in order.

In November 1991, Henry, heart-broken and unemployed, decided to go and live with his sister in Rock Hill, South Carolina. Soon after, he moved to his mother's home in nearby Charlotte, North Carolina. Wallace had been accused of rape. Whether it was the reason for him leaving Rock Hill is not clear, but in moving to Charlotte, once again his mother was in total control of Wallace's life. What she, the family, and the authorities did not know was that Wallace had already begun the murderous campaign that would make him North Carolina's most prominent serial killer.

TWO

Getting Started

When Wallace got out of the service in August 1989, and before he left for Charlotte, he had moved back in with his mother in Barnwell. He was happy to see wife Maretta and the sex was like the sex he had when they were first married. He was having sex two or three times a day, every day, but then, for some reason after the Christmas holidays, the sex became almost non-existent. When Wallace asked Maretta why they weren't having sex anymore. Maretta got enraged and snapped at Wallace, "Is that all you want from me?" Wallace said no, but he pointed out that they had not had sex in three weeks. She told him if he wanted sex he could get it elsewhere. Wallace said he did not want it that way.

Then one day in late December they had sex, but Wallace could tell Maretta was not into it. He asked her: "When we are having sex, do you visualize the rapist having sex with you?" She told him yes. Wallace was upset. He got up from the bed, showered, put on his clothes, and went for a walk. He thought about committing suicide.

It got to the point where Wallace and Maretta did not speak to each other. As Wallace later explained, "If she wore something like an outfit that was kind of revealing, or if I looked at her and said, 'you know, your legs look very nice,' she would get up and put on a long coat or something, cover herself up. And what could I do?"

The illegitimate child born by Maretta Brabham to another man through rape before her marriage to Henry Wallace had become a problem in their marriage. Maretta was raped, but she bore the child anyway. Wallace had a lot of anger about the rape, and he thought of finding the man who had raped Maretta so he could kill him. But she didn't want to talk about it. Maretta would not tell Henry anything about the man: not his name, who he was, or where he worked, even though Henry surmised she had all that information.

Wallace was stunned and hurt when Maretta revealed to him that when she had sex, she visualized her rapist raping her. Wallace later told police investigators, "It hurt me really, really, really bad, and I started thinking about when I was a child and my neighbor was raped and strangled. It kept playing back in my mind." Wallace was infuriated when he learned that she had never reported the rape. Wallace revealed he tried to commit suicide then, but failed.

Wallace's relationship with his wife got worse, to the point where he could not touch or kiss her. Even if he tried, she would get up and go sleep in another room. Wallace was never able to touch Maretta again.

Wallace said he desperately tried to make his marriage work. "Even before the first person was killed, I cried out to my wife," he explained to police investigators. "I cried out to her day after day, let's make this thing work. We took an oath in front of God to make it work. I don't know what in heaven and earth I did to that woman to make her turn against me the way she did. I lost all trust, all hope."

Earlier in 1990, with his marriage on the rocks, 25-year-old Henry Wallace had reconnected with an 18-year-old pretty dark-eyed high school senior named Tashanda Bethea from Barnwell. Wallace had fantasized sexually about the girl, although he claimed he did not do it in a violent manner. In Barnwell's intimate setting, Wallace had known Bethea and her family for most of his life. Wallace's mother had worked with Bethea's mother at the same factory and they were friends. Bethea had lived with her aunt and uncle in the same Barnwell neighborhood as the Wallace family. Wallace evidently had a crush on Bethea and wanted to date her.

Despite Wallace's mother's tyrannical ways, Henry had managed to get access to the family car and was able to get close to Bethea by offering her rides. The two had a friendly relationship and chatted with each other amicably when together. The two even dated, despite Henry being seven years older. One night, they made out, but Bethea said she did not want to have sex with him and Henry backed off.

Henry felt that he had spent a lot of time with Bethea, but had gotten nothing in return. Henry later told FBI Profiler Robert Ressler that he took the anger from that moment, locked it away, and waited for the moment when he would get payback.

That happened on March 18, 1990, when Henry was driving in his car and spotted Bethea walking down a country road to a school baseball game. Henry slowed down and drove up beside Bethea. In his suave manner, Wallace asked her where she was going. Bethea said she was going to the baseball game. Henry offered to drive her there, but she asked where he was going. He said to pick up something. He asked her if she wanted to come along. "Why not," Bethea said.

Wallace drove her out to the city limits and to a heavily forested area where he told Bethea that he needed to get out of the car to go to the bathroom. Wallace now had a change of plans. He relieved himself and then returned to the car where he took out a .357 revolver from the trunk, pointed the gun at her, and told her to get out of the car. He ordered her to take off her clothes, then he raped her on the hood of the car. When Wallace was finished, he had Bethea dress again.

After Wallace raped Bethea, he reportedly asked if she would tell anyone. At first she said yes, but then became scared and said she wouldn't tell. But it was too late. Wallace feared that Bethea would report the crime, so he decided to kill her.

In his later confession to police investigators, he described how he did it. He tried to choke her in the back seat of the car. After Bethea revived, he attempted to strangle her a second time. Then he slashed her wrists and throat with a box cutter and threw her into a pond. This all happened about six miles outside Barnwell. An autopsy performed after the body was discovered two weeks later concluded Bethea was still alive when she was thrown into the water. To cover his tracks, Wallace thoroughly cleaned and vacuumed the vehicle.

When Bethea did not return home, her family realized something was wrong and began looking for her. Nobody had seen her. She had disappeared. The family filed a missing person report with the Barnwell County Sheriff's Office the night she went missing.

Several people said they saw Wallace with Bethea. The Barnwell County Police Department took Wallace in and questioned him for hours. Wallace, however, remained composed under questioning. "We suspected that he was guilty, but we couldn't break him," recalled Ed Carroll, a former sheriff of Barnwell County who was one of the officers questioning Wallace. "He willingly answered the questions, but we could tell there was untruth in his voice. But we had to let him go."

Forensic experts combed Wallace's car for traces of blood, hair, or fibers from Bethea's clothing, but found nothing. Wallace remained one of three or four suspects in the case who had been seen with Bethea, so the Barnwell Police Department remained suspicious of Wallace and frustrated they could not arrest him. Then nearly two weeks later, on April 1, two fishermen found Bethea's body floating in a pond outside of town. The police hoped to find some solid evidence, but the young girl had been in the water too long and any evidence that could have tied Wallace to the murder had been washed away. "Water does terrible things to DNA," Carroll noted.

The police combed Wallace's car for traces of blood, hair, and fiber, but found nothing. They concluded that Wallace had thoroughly cleaned and vacuumed the vehicle.

The Barnwell police continued to investigate the case even though it taxed the department's limited resources. Finally, the department had to let go and the Tashanda Bethea murder became a cold case. "We would have liked to put Wallace under surveillance, but we didn't have the manpower," Carroll noted.

The Tashanda Bethea case would establish a pattern with Wallace's later murders. The murders were always the same. The victims would be Black and in the same age range. And somehow there was always a personal connection. It would make Henry Wallace one of the first serial killers who knew all his victims. The claim that he was first is incorrect. Jerry Marcus, an African American serial killer who murdered seven women in the late 1970s and the 1980s, knew all his victims. In much the same manner as Henry Wallace, Marcus used charm to hide his murderous intentions.

Later, when Wallace became the notorious serial killer of several women in Charlotte, he became the suspect in two criminal cases in South Carolina. The first one was the May 1987 murder of Pernetta Riddle of Allendale, South Carolina. The murder has never been solved. Riddle, who was thirty at the time and worked as a nurse in a private home, was found strangled in her apartment. Riddle had been dead for a day and half when her body was found by the apartment manager.

Lucile Mew believed that money was the motive for the murder. Riddle had just gotten her income tax refund, but police did not find one dollar on her. "It turned the whole family upside down," Lucile Mew, Riddle's older sister, told the *State* newspaper in Colombia. "My mother has never recovered. Ever since then, she doesn't know what day or month it is."

Allendale Police Chief James Grant noted that Riddle was strangled with one of her headbands in a manner resembling the Charlotte murders for which Wallace was charged. The Chief further noted that Wallace was on leave from the navy about the time Riddle was killed.

Eartha Brown, then 16, a sophomore at Barnwell High School and a friend of Tashanda Bethea, reported to police that Wallace had held a gun to her head and tried to rape her on March 31, 1990. Wallace had picked her up and they went to a hotel where Wallace said he was going to steal a television set. Brown, meanwhile, went into the hotel to use the bathroom.

In an interview with the *State* newspaper, Brown revealed what happened next. "I got out of the bathroom, and he grabbed me from behind and tried to tear the clothes off me. Then he put a gun to my head and said he was going to kill me. I kept screaming and stuff, (sic) and then he stopped. He put me back in his car and drove me home."

Brown said she was scared to say anything, but her mother went to the Allendale police and swore out a warrant. It was the same day that Tashanda Bethea's body was found. Wallace was arrested, questioned, but, remarkably, released eight days later.

There was also a rape in Allendale in 1991 that may have had a connection to Wallace. A woman called the Allendale Police Department, claiming she was positive that Wallace was the man who raped her in a doctor's office. Wallace was also questioned in the rape of a 14-year-old Barnwell teen, but he wasn't charged in that case either.

Bad Henry just could not avoid conflict with the law. On February 20 and 21, police in Barnwell County charged Wallace with larceny and third-degree burglary after he was convicted of breaking into Barnwell High School and the WDOG radio station. He served four months in state prison. The heat got too much for Henry Wallace and he decided a change in scene was in order. That is when, in late 1991, after his release, Wallace moved in with his sister, Yvonne, in Rock Hill, South Carolina, but he could not stay out of trouble. He was suspected of rape in that city as well.

After a short stay with Yvonne, Henry, heartbroken from the breakup with his wife, unemployed, and the subject of law enforcement's attention, Wallace decided to move to his mother's home in Charlotte, North Carolina. Once again, his mother was in total control of Wallace's life.

Wallace later claimed to police investigators that he came to Charlotte for a better life. "I just wanted to change my life," he explained. "I wanted to have a better life. I wanted to become better. I wanted to be a good person. But unfortunately, being from a small town and coming to and living in a large city for the first time, not, you know, being on your own, not really having anybody. Maybe it was a bit much for me, especially when I started indulging in and experimenting with different drugs and what not. I just couldn't handle it."

By now, with Wallace in Charlotte, the Tashanda Bethea murder was considered a cold case. Wallace had avoided all accountability, and he would be helped as an emerging serial killer by the new environment in which he operated.

Wallace came to Charlotte when it was booming and growing by leaps and bounds. Between 1990 and 2015, the population of Mecklenburg County, in which Charlotte resided, doubled, surpassing one million residents. While many newcomers came from across the country, a growing number came from around the world, particularly Latin America. It reached the point that Nielsen Media Research ranked Charlotte the fastest growing Latin metropolis in the entire U.S. for the period from 2000 to 2013.

This growth helped to make Charlotte the most ethnically diverse city in North Carolina, according to a news report by the WalletHub. The national personal financial institution named Charlotte the 23rd most diverse city in the nation among cities with more than 300,000 residents.

To accommodate the growth of rapid urbanization, Charlotte built new schools, roads, and hospitals. As Charisse T.M. Coston and Joseph B. Kuhns III, professors at the University of North Carolina at Charlotte, wrote in their paper, *Lives Interrupted: A Case Study of Henry Wallace, an African American Serial Killer in a Rapidly Expanding Southern City*, "Charlotte was a modest size city that was experiencing a tremendous population surge when Henry Louis Wallace arrived in 1992. Any city that is experiencing rapid growth, significant population transition, and the social disorganization that ultimately results provides an ideal setting for a serial offender who is interested in staying under the radar."

Charlotte was becoming known as a business and financial hub, as well as a university town with a well-educated population. In terms of population, the city had entered the country's top twenty cities.

Economically, in 1994, the city was recognized as the sixth largest wholesale center in the country with $11 billion. Nearly 14,000 jobs were created in 1994 alone, and because of that, forecasters placed Charlotte eighth in the list of American cites destined to reach zenith economic growth over the next decade. Measured by control of assets, Charlotte was becoming the second largest banking headquarters in the United States after New York City.

The city was proud of its race relations. Nearly 36 percent of the city's population was Black. The proportion of African Americans living and working in the Charlotte area was more than twice as high as their proportion in the general U.S. population. For the most part, the city's Black urban culture coexisted well with whites.

Charlotte, however, had its problems, too. This was especially true with law enforcement. With rapid growth came an increase in crime. Charlotte had forty-two murders in 1990. Three years later that figure had shot up to more than a hundred, setting new homicide records. According to the FBI's Uniform Crime Reporting (UCR) Program, Charlotte-Mecklenburg stats for 1993 indicate there were more than 51,000 incidences of crime, 9,102 of these falling under the description of "violent." Broken down, they included 87 murders, 350 rapes, 2,713 robberies, and 5,952 assaults. This was disturbing, indicating that, while crime was reportedly leveling off across the country, it was still on the rise in Charlotte. Charlotte police were investigating a murder almost every day and they were doing it with only seven detectives.

Journalist Frye Gaillard wrote in the January 1996 issue of the *Charlotte Magazine*: "If you made a target in the shape of Mecklenburg County, most homicides would hit the bull's eye—the poor neighborhoods in the inner city. But the terror of it spread to other parts of town. People heard about the killings and felt unsafe. With body count rising on the TV news, murder became the ultimate symbol of crime—and a city that seemed to be losing control."

In addition to being understaffed, the Charlotte-Mecklenburg Police Department (CMPD) operated on a shoestring budget. It was ill equipped and inexperienced to deal with a savvy serial killer who operated under the radar as Wallace did. Consequently, it simply failed to connect the various murders committed by Wallace.

In their defense, police claimed that they lacked financial and manpower resources. At the time, CMPD had outdated computers and, as earlier noted, only assigned seven homicide detectives to handle a heavy workload.

During 1993, moreover, Charlotte also experienced their highest number of homicides in a year (122) of which 94 of the homicide victims were Black. "We were faced with the crack epidemic," Garry McFadden, retired CMPD detective who headed the Wallace investigation, told *Fox News.* "A lot of people were getting robbed. A lot of homes were getting broken into. Purse snatching, carjacking, shootings, missing persons because they were on drugs—there was lot of crime, a lot of chaos."

Glenn Counts, a news reporter for Charlotte's WSOC television station, an NBC affiliate, agreed that the CMPD faced serious staffing issues at the time. "Charlotte was becoming a big city, but it still had a smaller city mentality when it came to policing," Counts explained. "The way it was being done in 1993 was the way it had always been done, even though Charlotte was rapidly changing."

And as Charisse T.M. Coston and Joseph B. Kuhns III, explain in *Lives Interrupted*, "Local homicide detectives further noted that his initial cleverness and meticulous attempts to remove and destroy evidence made Wallace particularly difficult to identify and apprehend. In other words, if Wallace had not become careless, the victim total could have probably been much higher."

Ironically, in perusing Wallace's murderous intentions, it helped him that he is Black. Historically, one of the criminal myths has been that serial killers are white. In researching his book, *The Rise of Black Serial Killers: Documenting a Startling Trend,* writer Justin Contrell debunked this myth. He uncovered the fact that Black serial killers have never represented less than 30.23 percent of the number of serial killers in a given decade, despite their overall percentage of the population never exceeding 13.1percent. It didn't help in the Wallace crime spree that all of his victims were Black. Historically, there has been a perception in the African American community that law enforcement tends to ignore Black female victims of violent crime.

"Charlotte provided an opportunistic environment where a meticulous serial murderer could operate in relative obscurity and continually escape detection," Charisse

T.M. Coston and Joseph B. Kuhns III explained in *Lives Interrupted.*

When the FBI released its annual crime report in early October 1993, it revealed that the seven-county Charlotte metropolitan area ranked eleventh in the rate of violent crime, which put it up there with the larger metropolises of New York City, Los Angeles, Miami, and Chicago. In 1992, Charlotte, for cities of 100,000 (excluding surrounding counties), ranked 20th in violent crime, a high figure when you consider Charlotte is the country's 35th largest city. In 1993, Charlotte had 2,388 murders, rapes, and aggravated assaults per 100,000 population, a disturbingly high number.

Wallace moved into East Charlotte, a thriving area with a population of more than 50,000 residents and boasting the then-prosperous Eastland Mall. He settled in the Glen Hollow Apartments on Central Avenue and later at the Granville Apartments on North Sharon Amity Road. There were plenty of restaurants, especially the fast-food variety, which offered ample work for cooks, dishwashers, waiters, and waitresses. Wallace worked as a cook or assistant manager at Taco Bell, Bojangles, Captain D's, and the Black Eye Pea near Eastland Mall.

With his charming personality, Wallace was able to make friends easily. People never saw the other side, the Mr. Jekyll to the Dr. Hyde, of his personality. "He was such a charmer," recalled Dee Sumpter. Her daughter, Shawna Mack, would be one of his victims. "He was well mannered and soft spoken. He didn't look like Denzel Washington, but he had a way with women."

By the time he came to Charlotte, it was clear that Wallace had a persistent drug problem. He had been a drug user of cocaine, LSD, and marijuana since the age of sixteen, given his own recollection. He told a neuropsychologist in May of 1996 that he did cocaine every day from 1993 through 1994. Wallace reported to a neurologist that he had smoked marijuana three or four times a week from age 13 to

28. During this time, he drank alcohol the most in his life. He reported that he was drinking sixteen to eighteen beers a day and a fifth of liquor per day from age 26 to 28.

Later he described to police investigators how he became hooked on drugs, "…it was like I was just smoking marijuana (when) I met someone here (Charlotte) who introduced me to powdered cocaine. I started doing lines, and one particular night, when my girlfriend was asleep, I was doing lines, and then had a bowl, and I had some marijuana, and I put some pot on top, and I heated it with some fire. That was all she wrote."

In Charlotte, Wallace also began to smoke crack cocaine, the habit becoming increasingly central to his life. In the early 1990s, crack was ravaging Charlotte. "Crack cocaine was having a major impact on Charlotte in the early 1990s. No question," Counts says. "The city got much more violent. A lot of the crime was bad guy on bad guy, but the average citizen was affected. The police did not have the resources to deal with the surge."

According to Counts, the CMPD was as good at protecting the public as they were allowed to be under the circumstances. "On any given day, you had up to five homicide detectives working dozens of cases," Counts explains. "They never had a chance to seriously investigate a case before they were on to the next case and the next case and the next."

Wallace's life in Charlotte did not go well at first. He was fired from several different fast-food restaurants before ending up working at a local Taco Bell. Wallace worked hard and was promoted to manager. But he continued his crack cocaine habit and it was making him reckless and careless. He impregnated one of his girlfriends, although he was delighted to be a father.

It was during this time that Wallace began his murder campaign in Charlotte. In May 1992, he picked up Sharon Nance, a 33-year-old reputed prostitute and convicted drug dealer. Despite her tough background, Nance's family knew her as a kind woman who drew, wrote poetry, and loved her son.

Garry McFadden, now the Mecklenburg County Sherriff, knew Sharon Nance. "She was one of the first people I met when I came to Charlotte," McFadden recalled, "She was living on the streets at the time. She was standing at a bus stop in the rain. I'm a southern gentleman, so I gave her an umbrella and walked off. I saw her a couple of times after that. We talked and became friends. She was very nice. Sharon's sister eventually came to work for me."

McFadden remembers Nance as having a beautiful smile and laughing a lot. "It was heartbreaking," McFadden told *Fox News*. "Her lifestyle complicated things, but I think we need to look at it from a different perspective. She was a person who was loved. She was a human being. So, no matter what her lifestyle is like, she was still someone's daughter. I think we need to look at that more closely, especially law enforcement when they are investigating these cases. Don't judge the victim by their profession or lifestyle."

Relatives say Nance fell in with a bad crowd, started using drugs, and got into trouble. Police records show she faced 61 charges between 1975 and 1992, including minor traffic offenses, assault, and drug and weapon charges. She had recently been released from prison.

To Nance's family, she was a sweet woman who loved her son. "Whatever she could do for somebody, she would do it," recalled Linda Nance, her sister. Another sister, Doris Black, remembered Sharon. "Regardless of what she had ever done, she was the best person I ever knew."

In May 1992, Sharon Nance left her aunt's house, wearing a black dress. She said she was going out with friends. When Sharon never returned home, the family instinctively knew that the worst had happened to Sharon.

A week later, TV reports showed images of police finding a woman's body in a black dress.

Wallace had picked Nance up and an argument ensued. Nance was believed to have wanted payment for sex. Wallace blew up. He grabbed Nance and began beating her. When she resisted, he beat her to death.

Later, Wallace told police investigators he could not remember Nance's name. As Wallace explained the murder, "We had sexual intercourse. She demanded money, and I didn't have any money, and we got into a scuffle, and it turned into basically me beating her to death."

Wallace dumped the body on a road next to the railroad tracks near the 5800 block of Rozelles Ferry Road. The body was discovered a week later. Police determined that Nance was not killed at the location, but had been dumped there. They found little forensic evidence. They learned that Sharon may have been a sex worker, which greatly increased the suspect pool. That Nance's sister sex workers were not talking with the police made the investigation more difficult. Indeed, no witnesses came forward.

The investigation into Nance's murder quickly cooled and nothing ever came of her killing. The police never conducted a serious investigation and Nance's death was never classified as a murder.

Wallace had easily avoided a murder charge in Barnwell. Now, the Charlotte police had no clue what had happened to Sharon Nance in Charlotte. Wallace's confidence and belief that he could get away with murder had grown. As Ann Burgess explained in her book, *Killer by Design,* "He felt like he could get away with anything he wanted. He felt infallible."

The following month, Wallace would strike again.

THREE

Reckless Times

In Charlotte, Wallace continued his reckless behavior. He had difficulty keeping a job and was fired from several fast-food restaurants. Wallace's inability to stay employed is largely attributed to his continued heavy use of drugs. In addition to cocaine and marijuana, he was now into crack cocaine. Still, Wallace was able to not only hide his heavy drug use from his family, but also his inner vehemence from the world. "The very people he killed trusted him," explained Charisse Coston, Professor of Criminal Justice at the University of North Carolina, who interviewed Wallace several times. "They had no forewarning of their death, even seconds before he struck at them."

The smooth-talking Wallace always seemed to find another job. He ended up as manager of a Taco Bell where he continued to project to the people he met the image of an amiable nice guy. He would offer to help people fix things around the house and provide them with rides to work or school. He would listen to their problems and give them advice on their relationships. His charm helped him make friends easily. Women viewed him as a kind of big brother in whom they could trust and confide. Some of Wallace's acquaintances even referred to him as "Uncle Henry."

What they did not know was that Wallace was a ruthless predator who watched and waited for the right opportunity to stage an attack. When women were alone with Wallace, they did not know the monster with whom they were dealing.

Wallace had moved in with a young woman named Sadie McKnight who appeared not to know the man behind the façade that Wallace presented to the public. Wallace managed to get a girlfriend pregnant in December 1992, while living with McKnight.

Wallace continued his drug use, heavily partaking in crack cocaine. Wallace was becoming part of a nationwide trend. By 1980, reports of crack use were appearing in Los Angeles, San Diego, Houston, and the Caribbean. Between 1984 and 1990, there was surge of crack cocaine use across the country. By 1987, crack was reported to be available in North Carolina and all but four states in the country. By 1990, the use of crack cocaine had reached epidemic proportions in this country, and the city of Charlotte was no exception. In addition to its cheapness, crack use reached epidemic proportions during the early 1990s because it was readily available and produced an immediate and intense euphoria in its user.

Crack was the common man's drug, purer and much cheaper than the traditional illicit drugs on the market. An average rock of cocaine could be bought for a mere $10. Moreover, it could be easily made.

Crack was largely blamed as the catalyst for the tremendous increase in crime from 1988 to 1993. Charlotte went from 48 murders in 1988 to 80 in 1989. By 1991, there were 121 murders. Two years later, there were 129 people killed in Charlotte, the most ever in the city's history. Violent crime in general spiked as well, up 16 percent between 1989 and 1993.

Wallace lived with McKnight and her roommate, Caroline Love, a co-worker at a local Bojangles on Central Avenue. She had attended Garinger High School and studied nursing at Central Piedmont Community College.

She also ran track at Northeast Junior High School. She had begun work at the Bojangles in September 1989 and had been there until June 1992. A Charlotte native, Love had been a Bojangles' restaurant cashier for two and a half years. Caroline Love is remembered as a warm, loving, and trusting person.

She would stroll into the Bojangles everyday wearing her headphones and playing her favorite rap music. She was always on time, even though she was going to school. "She was a vibrant woman who was living life," recalled Garry McFadden, who, at the time, was a CMPD sergeant before heading the Wallace investigation. "She just befriended the wrong person."

"Love was an excellent worker," Terry Bizakis, who was her manager, remembered in a *Charlotte Observer* interview: "She did her job. Never gave me any problems. She could stretch out and pick up a little extra and never really complain about it."

Wallace admitted to criminal profiler Ann Burgess that he fantasized about raping Love. He was obsessed with the young girl and could not stop thinking about her.

On June 15, 1992, Love left her apartment and went to work. Bojangles was close, so she walked. At work, she asked her manager if she could change ones for quarters, which she planned to use at the laundromat after her shift ended. The manager agreed and Caroline left work, walking home. On the way, she ran into her cousin Robert who offered to drive her home. Love accepted. Robert watched as she entered the apartment.

Earlier that day, Wallace was at the apartment because his girlfriend, Sadie McKnight, was Love's girlfriend and roommate. McKnight had cleaned the apartment. She had left her house key on the wall. When McKnight was not looking, Wallace took the key, made a copy, and put it back on the wall without McKnight noticing.

Later that day, Wallace was driving around when he decided to stop at his girlfriend's apartment. When Love arrived home, she was surprised to see Wallace in her apartment, but she was not worried. After all, Wallace was her friend, her roommate's boyfriend. He was harmless, or so she thought.

He had let himself into her apartment using the key he had made from the key owned by girlfriend Sadie McKnight. Wallace said he was in the bathroom and would leave as soon as he came out. When Wallace came out of the bathroom, he went into the living room where Caroline was watching television.

Wallace came up to Love and gave her a kiss on the cheek. Love did not like it. She asked Wallace why he had kissed her. He did not really have a good answer. She told Wallace that if he promised not to do that again, she wouldn't tell his girlfriend about it. Wallace blew up and attacked Love, violently putting her in a chokehold, which he would later describe to police as the "Boston choke."

Love fought back, scratching Wallace on the arms, face, hands, neck, and the back of the head. Wallace kept applying the chokehold on Love until she was barely conscious. He then dragged her to the bedroom, removed her clothes, and raped her while continuing to apply the chokehold. Love continued struggling during the rape. Wallace reached for the nearest object, a curling iron. He took the cord to the iron and tightened it around Love's neck until she passed out.

Wallace then moved Love to her bedroom. He removed her clothes, tied her hands behind her back with the cord of the curling iron, and placed tape over her mouth. Love remained semi-conscious as Wallace had oral sex then sexual intercourse with her. Love began to regain consciousness, so Wallace continued to apply the chokehold until her body became limp. When Wallace felt Love's heart and pulse and realized she was still alive, he proceeded to strangle her to death.

Why did Wallace suddenly murder Love? Wallace later explained: "Caroline and my girlfriend had been over to my apartment on several occasions, and they use (sic) to always kind of tease me, and we would all three get on the floor and have little wrestling matches. And I remember one particular time Caroline had come over. She had on some shorts, and I—she was kind of attractive to me. She hit me in the groin area pretty hard, and that kind of ended that little play session. But I don't know…at that particular time I saw her with the shorts on, from that day forward she was kind of attractive to me."

But Wallace had not been thinking. He did not realize that he would have to get rid of the body and that would mean hauling it out of the apartment. He worried that somebody would see him. There was a white man who lived in the apartment directly behind Sadie's and Caroline's apartment. On several occasions, when Wallace and his girlfriend Sadie were in the apartment, the neighbor would stand on the patio and look at their apartment through his window. Wallace worried that the man might see him.

Ever the risk taker, Wallace decided to chance it. He wrapped Love's body in a blanket and left the apartment. He moved his car closer to the stairwell. He then returned to the apartment with a large orange trash bag. Wallace placed some clothes in another bag to make it seem that Love had left the apartment. Wallace wrapped Love's corpse in her bed sheets, stuffed her into the trash bag, and dragged her out to his car where he placed the trash bag in the back seat.

Nobody had noticed. He returned to the apartment, grabbed the roll of quarters that Love had meant to use for the laundry, and locked the door. He then drove the vehicle through Charlotte's streets trying to find a place to dump the body. He drove down Statesville Road, removed the bag containing Love's body from the car, and dumped it in the woods.

The following day, Wallace returned to the scene of the crime because he believed the orange bag would be noticed from the road. He removed Love's body from the orange trash bag and moved it into a shallow ravine. In all, a nervous Wallace returned four times to the site where he had dumped Love.

Sadie McKnight returned to her apartment that night and got a call from Kathy Love, Caroline's sister. Where was Caroline, Kathy wanted to know? Caroline's supervisor at Bojangles had been looking for her because she had missed a shift. McKnight had no clue where Caroline was, but she realized it was unusual for Caroline not to check in with her for so long.

Love and McKnight went to the Charlotte-Mecklenburg police station and filed a missing person's report. They were accompanied to the station by none other than McKnight's boyfriend, Henry Wallace. Later, Kathy Love would search Caroline's apartment for clues as to her disappearance. She noticed that sheets from Love's bed were missing and that some of the furniture had been moved. The police did their own investigation and did not find much, other than the fact that the roll of quarters she had taken from work was missing from her apartment.

Investigators declared that Love's apartment bore suspicious signs, such as furniture that seemed disrupted during a scuffle, missing bed sheets, and a missing roll of quarters with which she was to do laundry. But her laundry hamper was full. She had not gone out to do laundry.

Sister Kathy continued to check to see if Caroline had gone to work. She had not. What had happened to Caroline? The Love family was desperate to know. But to the Love family's disappointment, the investigation ended there. Although no interview with Wallace is recorded in the investigation, somehow the CMPD concluded that Wallace had nothing to do with Love's disappearance. Love was declared a missing person. The case was filed away.

Two days later, Wallace returned to the spot where he had dumped the body. He described Love's body as being "decayed to the point where she just looked like a leather E.T. doll, or something." On his third visit, he found only bones. Wallace felt confident that no one would be able to identify Love even if they found her body. Meanwhile, no longer having a roommate, McKnight moved in with her boyfriend, Henry Wallace.

How did Love's murder impact Wallace's relationship with his girlfriend Sadie McKnight? When asked by the police investigator if Love's murder brought him closer to Sadie, Wallace responded: "In a sense it did, but in a way it didn't. It brought us closer because Sadie needed someone more—someone to, you know, someone there for her in her time of need, and I was there for her. But, at the same time, I was kind of hurting inside, and I felt yucky inside because I was the one who did the harm to her friend, and she had no idea."

Love was the third woman to go missing in Charlotte in the summer of 1992. Earlier, police had searched abandoned houses in Charlotte's Five Points area west of uptown for clues to the disappearances. Police and local residents feared that the women had been murdered and their bodies dumped in a vacant house. Love was missing for about a month before her story made its way into the media. Family and friends said it was out of character for her to be gone so long and not contact anyone.

In July 1992, the police finally appealed to the Charlotte community for help in finding the women. A second appeal went out two months later. Eventually, one of the women was found to be living in Atlanta. The second woman's body was discovered in some woods outside Charlotte. What happened to Caroline Love would remain a mystery for another two years. Meanwhile, seven months passed, and Wallace continued to live with McKnight.

Twenty-year-old Shawna Hawk was watching one of the television reports on the Caroline Love disappearance and she thought it odd that Caroline had disappeared and not contacted her family. Caroline was close to her family and would have been in touch with them. Shawna was the second child of Dee Sumpter and Walter Hawk, Jr. who were divorced. Her brother lived with the father, a high school principal in Atlanta, Georgia, while Shawna's older brother served in the military in Germany.

Shawna was living with her mother in East Charlotte in a two-story apartment on Elon Avenue. Back then, Dee Sumpter worked as a receptionist at a downtown law firm. Mother and daughter settled into a pleasant life in a quiet neighborhood that they thought was safe.

Shawna loved children and she helped take care of her godson, Jermond Williams II. Jermond's mother, Tasha Williams, and Shawna had met at East Mecklenburg High School and were good friends. On the day of her murder, Shawna was planning to pick up Tasha and Jermond but she never arrived.

Shawna was known to family and friends as the "Purple Princess" because purple was her favorite color. An ambitious young woman, she attended Central Piedmont Community College where she was studying law to become a paralegal. Shawna had been working since age 14 to help her mother pay the bills and she had given some of her checks to her mother even though her mother tried to give them back. Shawna was a good child.

She worked at nearby Taco Bell on Sharon Amity Road. Henry Wallace, the manager, had hired her, and they had known each other for five or six months. He offered to pay her $7 an hour, which was more than she had been paid at her other fast-food jobs.

Shawna and Wallace became good friends and even dated. Sumpter remembers one time when Wallace took Shawna to a comedy show. Sumpter recalls telling Wallace, "Take good care of her. Bring her back safely."

Sumpter liked Wallace. "He was a charmer, very likeable," Sumpter recalled. "He always acted as a gentleman, respectful, well-mannered and soft spoken." Sumpter remembers chatting with Wallace and being impressed. "He said, 'Nice to meet you, Miss Sumpter. I think Shawna is going to be great on our team.'"

Wallace says that Shawna was a very pretty girl, but claims he had no sexual attraction toward her. He thought she would make "the perfect wife type."

Family and friends remember Shawna as smart, pretty, and a kind person. She shared her mother's petite stature, vivaciousness, smooth skin, and sparkling blue eyes. Family members describe Shawna as her mother's best friend.

"Shawna was so easy going," recalled Walter Hawk, her brother. "She always avoided that tit for tat stuff. You could never get under her skin. I never saw her get into a fight with anybody. She cared about people. She made it her mission in life to care about the people she loved. I don't know how she did it, but she did."

The family was protective of Shawna. "We vetted the men who came into her life," Hawk said. "We would sit them down and tell them they had to treat her right."

Shawna and her mother had a special relationship. "Mom was more than Shawna's mother. She was her best friend," Hawk revealed. "Shawna would call her mother 'Dee'."

"I thought she was gorgeous," recalled Darrell Kirkpatrick who at the time was her boyfriend. "She was quiet, laid back, with a great sense of humor. We just hit it off."

Kirkpatrick was acting in a gospel play being performed at a theater. Dee Sumpter handled public relations for the theater. Shawna would come by the theater and observe. Eventually Shawna and Darrell started talking and getting to know each other.

On February 18, 1993, Kirkpatrick returned to Charlotte from Florida where he had visited his son. He accepted the invitation to stay for the weekend at the Sumpter home. The next morning Kirkpatrick woke up to find Shawna getting ready for school. He went into the bathroom and sat on the toilet while she took a shower. They talked until Shawna finished showering. Shawna got dressed and left the house for school. Kirkpatrick jumped back into bed and slept for about an hour. He woke up, got dressed, and left the house, expecting to spend a routine day. Shawna called Darrell when she had a break. Darrell told her he would come by the house later.

On the afternoon of Feb. 19, 1993, Shawna Hawk had just returned from classes at her community college. Hawk was slipping off her coat when she heard the doorbell ring. It was her manager from Taco Bell, Henry Wallace. Wallace and Hawk had a relationship that extended beyond work. As noted earlier, they were friends who would sometimes hang out together in their free time. Shawna trusted Wallace, so she let him in.

They chatted, and everything was fine until she began to tease him about a recent argument he had with his girlfriend, Sadie McKnight. Wallace had already felt some resentment toward Shawna. She would make fun of Wallace before her mother, and that embarrassed and angered Wallace. He had told her to stop, but she continued.

Wallace later told investigators that she had found out some information about him. That information related to a female with whom he had a child. "Once I was visiting Shawna (and) she teased me about that particular incidence and just kind of made fun of me in front of her mom, which kind of very upset me," Wallace told police investigators. "And I asked her on several occasions not to do it because it was offensive to me, and, you know, she thought it was kind of funny."

Shawna got Wallace a drink and they talked for about half an hour to forty-five minutes. Then they watched some television together. He was about to leave when Shawna gave Wallace a hug and a kiss on the cheek. They embraced and held each other tight.

At this point, Wallace later recalled, "That other side (of me), bam, it was there." It was like…a switch being turned on or a button being pushed or a door being opened."

Wallace told Shawna he wanted to have sex with her. Shawna asked Wallace if he was joking. Wallace told her no and ordered her to the bedroom.

Wallace shoved her into the bedroom and forced her to take off her clothes. Frightened, Hawk began to cry. She was afraid. She knew she was about to be raped. She cried continually through the ordeal. Wallace made her take off her panties and shoes. He made her have oral sex with him and then he had oral sex with her. He had sex with her in several different positions. When he finished, he told her to put her clothes back on.

Hawk started to pray, repeating the Lord's Prayer, and this made Wallace really scared. He decided he would have to kill Hawk or he would come to regret it.

Wallace then forced Hawk into the bathroom where he placed her head between his arms and put her in a chokehold. Shawna passed out. Later, Wallace told police investigators, "When I was administering the choke hold (sic), she never once put her hands to pry my arms from around her neck or anything. She just put her hands up in the air like that and then they started to drop down by her side."

Wallace filled the bathtub with water and put Shawna in it. He wanted to wash away hair fibers and body fluids that would be on her body. He submerged her in the water until she was dead. Wallace closed the curtains and left the bathroom door open to make it appear everything was normal. He took $50 of Hawk's money as he left the apartment.

Wallace took Hawk's car, a '78 or '79 Toyota Corolla, and drove it back to Central Piedmont Community College, where he parked the car in the lower level of the parking deck. Wallace caught a bus and went back home.

About 5 p.m. that day, Sumpter phoned Kirkpatrick and asked him if he had talked with Shawna. "Yeah, I talked with her earlier [that] day," Kirkpatrick revealed.

"I'm kind of worried," Sumpter said. "Her car is not here, but her stuff is. Her coat and purse are in a closet. It's cold outside. She never goes anywhere without her purse. I looked through Shawna's purse and noticed that her keys were not there. I think some money is missing, too."

Kirkpatrick felt helpless. He tried to reassure Sumpter. "She'll be back. Don't worry." Sumpter called Kirkpatrick again around 8 p.m. that night, frantic. "Where is Shawna?" Sumpter wanted to know. Kirkpatrick told her he would come right over.

When Kirkpatrick came over, they decided to look systematically through each room in the house. "I was kind of worried, but I didn't let on," Kirkpatrick revealed. "I was trying to keep Dee calm. I looked all around the house, even under Shawna's bed, but found nothing. I really didn't know what we were looking for. We eventually stopped looking and went into the living room and watched television. Dee was real upset. I felt helpless. I told her we should call the police. Dee agreed. We thought about filing a missing person report, but when we called the police, they said it hadn't been twenty-four hours, so there was nothing much they could do. So, we were sitting there, nervous, anxious. Then for some reason I got up and walked into the downstairs bathroom."

Kirkpatrick looked around. He noticed that the carpeting was soaked, and when he went into the bathroom, he noticed that the shower curtain was not tucked in place. Through the translucency of the curtain, Kirkpatrick thought he could see something or someone crouched behind the wall of the tub.

He pulled the shower curtain back. There was Shawna in the bathtub, curled up, and completely submerged in water. "I screamed and ran back to Dee," Kirkpatrick explained. "All I could say was: "Call the cops! Call the cops!""

Sumpter called the police. She was hysterical. When the police arrived, Sumpter was standing in the yard screaming. Kirkpatrick came out of the house, screaming, "Please hurry. You've got to do something. She is in the bathroom."

Kirkpatrick led the officer into the house and to the bathroom. The dark blue shower curtain was closed completely. Kirkpatrick pulled back the curtain so the officer could look inside the tub. Shawna was lying on her right side. Her knees were drawn up. She was in a semi-fetal position. Shawna's head was totally under the water. She was fully clothed. She wore a plain shirt, black jogging-type pants, and blue tennis shoes.

The fire department arrived and took Shawna out of the tub and laid her out in the hallway. The medics tried CPR on Shawna in a desperate effort to save her. Mother Dee cried and prayed that they would save Shawna.

FOUR

Trauma

It was too late. Shawna Hawk was pronounced dead at the hospital. The 240-pound Henry Wallace had choked the life out of petite 104-pound Shawna Hawk. Her skull had suffered lacerations and bruising caused by a blow from a dull and heavy object. However, while that object may have dealt unconsciousness, it had not killed her. The examining doctor diagnosed that she had been strangled to death.

On February 20, 1993, forensic pathologist Dr. James M. Sullivan performed an autopsy on Hawk's body. He noted hemorrhaging in the conjunctiva (lining of the eyes), the face, the lips, and across the voice box—all trademarks of ligature strangulation. So, based on his observations, Dr. Sullivan concluded that the cause of Hawk's death was ligature strangulation. According to Dr. Sullivan, a ligature is "a cord or a band, or something that's made into a cord or a band, then circles the neck and is used to forcibly compress the neck."

Sullivan indicated that based on the bruising present, the blow occurred prior to death but it was unlikely that the blow caused unconsciousness. He discovered a contusion on the left side of Hawk's scalp above the ear and a laceration of the left eardrum with some hemorrhaging behind the eardrum, evidence of a blunt trauma prior to death.

Based on Dr. Sullivan's autopsy, the authorities determined that Shawna's death was a homicide. Police were called in. The Hawk family asked the police if they had questioned classmates and co-workers. The police assured the family it had. The police had interviewed Wallace in their Caroline Love missing person investigation, but they could not find anything that indicated Wallace had anything to do with her disappearance. The police failed to come up with a suspect or a motive. They were stumped.

Suspicion fell on Darrell Kirkpatrick. After all, he was the last person to see Shawna alive. "I know the entire family thought I did it," Kirkpatrick recalls. "It was a very unsettling time for me. I loved Shawna."

Dee Sumpter confirms that her family suspected Kirkpatrick of killing Shawna. "Of course, you always suspect the persons closest to the victim, especially when you got no suspect," Sumpter acknowledged.

Judy Williams, Sumpter's good friend from elementary school days, even went to Kirkpatrick's mother's office and confronted Darrell. "Judy said to Darrell: 'I know you did it, so tell the truth,'" Sumpter recalled Williams saying to Kirkpatrick.

Sumpter, however, reached a different conclusion after studying Kirkpatrick for a while. "I remember meeting Darrell at Shawna's grave," she said. "He was in a million pieces, and he would always tell me how hurt he was. When I would tell him I'm going to Shawna's grave, he would be eager to meet me there. I would listen to him, watch him, and after a while, I removed him from my list of suspects. I knew he loved Shawna and would not kill her."

Meanwhile, Dee Sumpter had no doubt that Shawna knew who her killer was. Mentally she went through the people that Shawna knew; her friends and associates. She went over and over in her mind the names of people who might have killed Shawna but couldn't come up with a suspect. "I had a million questions swirling in my mind," she said. "I had to deal with it all day, every day."

She thought of Henry Wallace; sweet, kind Henry, the young man who seemed so considerate and caring of Shawna. Wallace had gone to Shawna's funeral. At the viewing, he was seen sitting all alone at the back of the room with a strange look on his face, just staring.

One day, Sumpter bumped into Wallace at a shopping center. He hugged Sumpter and told her how sorry he was to hear about Shawna. How thoughtful, Sumpter thought. She dismissed sweet Henry from her list of suspects.

The Charlotte Mecklenburg Police Department's (CMPD) detectives had scoured the Hawk house for clues. They found no damage to the door or window, no footprints near the windows. They concluded that she most definitely had let the killer into the house.

The CMPD homicide unit was stretched thin and it could not put a lot of resources into the case. It took more than a year for police to connect Shawna Hawk's murder to the other women and to figure out that someone was killing young Black women who had worked at the east side fast-food restaurants.

Dee Sumpter was devastated at her daughter's murder. She found it hard to wake up in the morning and go out and face the world. She felt constant pain. "I didn't try to live one day at a time," Sumpter recalled. "It was more like one minute at a time. If I made it from 2 p.m. to 2:05 p.m., it was an achievement. I spent the days that way because Shawna's murder was so overwhelming. I don't know how I made it through that period."

Sumpter ended up seeking therapy from a man she will not openly identify for the sake of his privacy. Let us call him Mr. James. He was a prominent Charlotte psychologist who is now deceased. "I would meet him at my job on my lunch hour," Sumpter recalled. "He came to our support group meeting and offered his services. He would talk with us and answer our questions, give us advice, and advise us how to live through the murders."

The killer knew what he was doing. He had been meticulous. He had gone through the house and wiped it clean of any evidence. There was no DNA. No fingerprints.

Eight weeks after Shawna's murder, her car was still missing, but the police got a break. A Central Piedmont Community College (CPCC) security guard noticed her car parked at the college. The police knew Shawna had been at school. Did the killer take the car? At this point, the police did not know. The police searched the car for evidence of how it got there and who drove it.

The seat was pushed all the way back. Shawna was 5' 2". The car was driven to the exact spot where Shawna parked her car every day at the college. Did the killer know enough about Shawna to bring her car back to the college and park it in the exact same spot she did? It was another question that begged an answer.

Sumpter's friend, Judy Williams, thought Sumpter needed a new purpose. Sumpter and Williams had known each other since elementary school. Williams' son, David Howard, was Sumpter's godson.

Williams was the eldest daughter of eight siblings and grew up poor in Charlotte's Brooklyn neighborhood. Williams eventually became a prominent anti-violence activist. She also became the mastermind behind the idea to create a National Purple-Ribbon Campaign which promoted the purple ribbon to be recognized nationally, and now internationally, as the color and symbol against violence. Williams would go on to receive the 2017 Charlottean of the Year Award and the 2019MLK Keeper of the Dream Award. Sadly, Williams passed away in October 2020 from cancer.

"Judy led a very active life," Sumpter recalled. "She was always driven by her goals, and could accomplish anything she set out to do. We were both busy, so we didn't see each other as much as we wanted. She would put her son David out of the house after they had arguments. He would come to stay at our house. Shawna would say: 'David is here. He is homeless again.' And we would laugh."

One Saturday shortly after Shawna's murder, Sumpter was in Williams' living room crying her eyes out. Williams told Sumpter she could not take her grief anymore, and Williams and Howard came up with the idea for a support group, which they called Mothers of Murdered Offspring (MOM-O). They held a press conference, which was attended by all the media in Charlotte, to announce the formation of Mothers of Murdered Offspring (MOM-O).

The first meeting was held on March 29, 1993, about five weeks after Shawna Hawk's murder, at a community center in West Charlotte. "Mothers showed up with various memorabilia from their dead offspring—pictures, blood-stained shirts, etc.," Sumpter recalled. "We agreed to meet weekly for a kumbaya experience, share stories, hug (sic) and be there for each other." The group is still going strong today.

At that time there were no organizations or support groups dedicated to helping families of murder victims cope with the pain, anger, and sudden devastation that they were forced to endure. The group has the dual mission: to always support families through the cycle of grief and devastation that murder causes and to created, and support programs and activities that focus on the prevention of violence, assist with funeral arrangements, candlelight vigils, balloon-release services, keepsakes, and other remembrance celebrations.

While supporting other victims' families, Sumpter also put pressure on the police. She began to advocate for changes to police department procedures, saying detectives were not doing enough to solve the murder cases of Shawna and the others. It was a tense relationship. She made some enemies on the force, but today, she says her organization and the department's homicide support group work together to help victims' family members cope.

A year after Shawna's death and there still was no progress in solving her daughter's murder. Sumpter thought the authorities were dragging their behinds. She would show up at police headquarters and pester the police. Why don't you talk with my daughter's friends and co-workers, she demanded?

McFadden says Sumpter had every right to be upset with the pace of the investigation into her daughter's murder. "She lost her daughter, and there was almost no progress in the investigation," McFadden recalled. "The families were very vocal about their dissatisfaction. They were frustrated. At the time, we didn't appreciate the families of the victims. But I'll tell you. That would not be the case today," McFadden blames the city management for not getting the resources it needed. "They just wouldn't do it," McFadden said." We still had the small-town image, but we had grown into a big city."

It took about a year after the resolution of the Wallace case before the CMPD got an increase in its manpower and access to more sophisticated technology. Today, the CMPD has twenty-two homicide detectives handling the same number of cases as it was handling in 1993 and 1994.

Sumpter decided to approach the killer directly. She wrote a letter, which was published in the media, asking the killer to turn himself into the authorities. The letter read:

"Dear Killer: I am the mother of Shawna Denise Hawk. I am writing to you because you murdered my only daughter in our home on February 19, 1993, between the hours of 1 p.m. and 5 p.m. It is so hard to believe that an entire year has gone by since that horrible Friday evening when Shawna's dead body was discovered in the bathtub where you put her. I do not hate you. What purpose would that serve? I do want you to come forth and confess to the horrible atrocity you have committed." –Dee Sumpter

Wallace, however, was not paying attention. His crack habit was getting worse and doing the drug was not cheap.

He was not making enough money at his job at the Taco Bell on Wendover Road to support his habit. He looked around at the people he knew. Who would have money or have access to money? He would occasionally smoke marijuana with Aubrey Spain, his 24-year-old manager at Taco Bell. He figured she would have access to the company vault. That would be a good way to get some money.

Spain had grown up in Bayboro, a tiny coastal town in South Carolina. She was the youngest daughter of six children. Her parents, Broughton and Mae Helen Spain, hated to see their daughter leave home for the big city, but they gave her their blessing. Spain had hoped to find a job working in computers but that didn't work out and she ended up at Taco Bell. The job barely paid minimum wage and she struggled with money. But, somehow, she managed to pay the bills.

She hung out with a group of young people. Two of the group's members were Henry Wallace and Shawna Hawk. Stephanie Cook, who worked with Spain, remembered her as always wanting to make people smile and laugh.

On June 24, 1993, Wallace showed up at Aubrey Spain's apartment. Later Wallace admitted that robbery was his motive for visiting Spain. Wallace had met Spain in February of 1992. They were both shift managers at the Taco Bell on Sharon Amity Road. Spain was pretty in a tomboy sort of way. She would play tennis and basketball with Wallace. They were very tight and would attend comedy clubs and mixers together.

The relationship cooled and they stopped seeing each other when Sadie McKnight became Wallace's girlfriend. Then eight months later, Spain came by and asked Wallace if he could give her some money to pay for an abortion. Wallace didn't loan Spain the money and she stopped speaking to him.

Wallace needed money and knew Spain was a shift manager at the Taco Bell with access to the store's safe. He was angry with her because he believed she had helped get him fired from his job. He found out Spain was on vacation and waited for her return.

Upon her return, Wallace went over to her apartment. Without a thought, she let her friend, Wallace, into the apartment. Wallace asked her if she wanted to smoke a joint. She said yes and Wallace went home to get a joint. He came back. They smoked a joint, drank some beer, chatted, and were having a good time.

Spain relaxed. Her guard was down. She was enjoying her time with her friend. They both continued to smoke marijuana and get high.

When Spain turned her back, Wallace made his move. He sprang and put Spain in his Boston chokehold. Then he threw her to the ground. She was terrified. Wallace demanded to know the combination. Spain said she did not know the combination. "What about the money in your personal bank account?" Wallace demanded. Spain said she had just returned from a vacation and had none. Wallace dragged her into the bedroom and raped her. She screamed in terror and begged Wallace not to hurt her. He raped her again.

Wallace ordered her to get dressed, although he later said he did not remember asking Spain to remove her clothes. He then put another chokehold on her. As she lay unconscious, he tied a shirt and a nightgown into a makeshift rope and strangled her to death. He dragged Spain's body to the shower where he washed off any evidence. He then hauled Spain's body to the bed where he laid it out.

Wallace found some underwear and a suit of one of Spain's ex boyfriends and placed the clothing in a basket right below her bed. He took the underwear and pulled some of the pubic hairs from Spain's vagina and put them in the underwear so it looked like the pubic hairs belonged to the one who had sex with her last.

Wallace placed Spain's body on the bed, turned her over on her side, and covered her up. He searched the apartment for money but could not find any. Wallace took Spain's keys and credit card. He then turned the lights out and put the air conditioner down to the lowest temperature it would go to so that her body would not deteriorate at a rapid rate of speed. He locked the door and left the apartment.

Wallace returned to her apartment later and made some phone calls to make it seem she was still alive. Wallace used the credit card to purchase gas on several occasions; not only for himself but for others. They had no clue that the credit card belonged to a woman Wallace had murdered.

On June 23, 1993, Spain was to report to work at 6:30 p.m. at the Taco Bell restaurant on Wendover Road, but she did not show. Spain was a dependable employee, but she had also failed to show up for work the next day; that is, two days in a row, June 23 and June 24, 1993. Spain's manager at Taco Bell sensed something was wrong. It was not like Spain to not just show up without calling in. The manager called her twice, but the calls went to voice mail. He left a message on her answering machine, but she never responded.

On June 24, 1993, the manager decided to cruise by Spain's apartment. He saw Spain's car in the parking lot, entered the apartment building, and knocked several times on her apartment door, but no one answered. The manager called Spain's sister and left a message, expressing his concerns. She never called back. He called 9-1-1, and thereafter police officers rode by Spain's apartment, periodically knocking on the door, but, again, no one answered.

On June 25, maintenance personnel from the apartment complex entered Spain's apartment through a sliding door. They discovered the body on the bed, the face distorted, eyes bulging, the body stiff from incipient rigor mortis. It was the body of Audrey Spain.

The manager again stopped by Spain's apartment on June 25. An officer informed him that they had discovered Spain dead in her apartment.

Forensic pathologist Dr. James Sullivan concluded that the cause of death was strangulation. Dr. Sullivan also observed hemorrhages in the conjunctiva, on the skin of the face, in the voice box, and in the muscles in the front of the neck, as well as minor blunt-trauma injuries, including a small facial abrasion, small linear abrasions on her right back and on the knee, and a small contusion over the right hip. After removing the ligature, Dr. Sullivan discovered a furrow, or mark, left by the ligature. There was a ligature made from a T-shirt and a bra around Spain's neck with the end of the T-shirt stuffed into her mouth.

Later, Garry McFadden, who would eventually head the Wallace Investigation, would try to explain the CMPD's inability to connect the dots in the Wallace case. "We worked under very difficult conditions," McFadden, now sheriff in Mecklenburg County, told the A & E True Crime blog. "We never had time to collaborate. We never had time to give [cases] a lot of attention."

In 1993, the crime rate in Charlotte was soaring. Yet the police were trying to handle the increase in murders with seven detectives and one supervisor. "We were not only trying to handle murders with that number of detectives, but we were also handling other crime as well, like kidnappings and assaults," McFadden explained. "We had to do paperwork with those crimes. We had to go court and testify. We might have to fly out of the city, and maybe be gone five or six days. Who picks up the work when those things happen?"

Additionally, the Wallace investigations were hampered by the fact that the killer wiped down surfaces and put items he wasn't sure he touched in the oven to evaporate any prints. Wallace made at least one of his victims shower to wash off DNA evidence.

Yet there were striking similarities in the Hawk and Spain cases, if the police would have noticed. Both victims knew each other. Both were young, attractive Black women working in fast-food restaurants. In fact, both had worked at the same Taco Bell for a time. Both were killed by ligature strangulation and both had been robbed of money. There was no sign of forced entry to their homes. Both of their bodies, moreover, had been washed clean of evidence. And they lived close to each other.

There was no effort by police to establish a pattern in the murders, no effort to see if the Hawk and Spain murders were connected, or if any recent murders in Charlotte were connected, for that matter. As the murders mounted, the CMPD continued to treat each brutal murder of a young Black woman as a separate case, with a different police investigator assigned to each case.

Ironically, the CMPD figured they had a prime prospect in the Shawna Hawk case. Darrell Kirkpatrick had gone to the hospital where he was told there was nothing they could do for Shawna. The police were there and Kirkpatrick was asked to go down to the police station the next morning. The police wanted to talk with him. Kirkpatrick agreed. The next morning, he went to the police station where he was interviewed by Garry McFadden of the Homicide Division.

"McFadden asked me, 'When was the last time you and Shawna had sex?'" Kirkpatrick recalled. "I said: 'I don't remember.' He jumped up and said: 'You don't remember the last time you fucked her?' He made me strip butt naked in the police station, all the police looking at me. They combed through my pubic hairs. It was humiliating. I would never do anything to Shawna. I loved the girl."

Kirkpatrick did not realize it at the time, but he had brushed with Henry Wallace. Kirkpatrick had gone with a friend to see an acquaintance for some marijuana. "We came back to the house and the friend said we should invite the guy we got the weed from to come over for a beer," Kirkpatrick recalled. He did.

"Later I realized the man was Henry Wallace."

Kirkpatrick also did not realize at the time that Shawna's family suspected he was Shawna's killer. "It was a strange time," Kirkpatrick recalled. "I know that when they organized Mothers of Murdered Offspring (MOM-O), I was never invited to any of their meetings."

It did not help that Wallace was not your typical serial killer. He was Black. He knew his victims. In normal homicide cases, Blacks are usually overrepresented, occupying a much larger proportion than they occupy in the Black population at large. This has been well documented.

But when it comes to serial killers, the serial killer is invariably thought of as being white, contrary to the evidence that has been collected. Researchers have identified 90 Black serial killers beginning in 1945, yet their notoriety and celebrity have been absent in the media. White serial killers like John Wayne Gacy, Jeffrey Dahmer, and Ted Bundy are well known to the public, but try to name one Black serial killer.

In his book, *The Rise of the Black Serial Killers,* writer Joseph Cottrell documents a startling trend, in effect destroying the myth that serial killers in America are predominately white. He shows through extensive research that the number of Black serial killers is equal to or greater than the number of white serial killers from 1860 to present.

Yet, law enforcement agencies might be less likely to seek or find evidence of serial murder activity where the victims are Black. As homicide is primarily an intra-racial crime, this would then mean that Black serial killers would be far more likely to escape detection.

Allan Branson in his article, "African American Serial Killers: Over-Represented Yet Under-Acknowledged," which appeared in the *Howard Journal of Crime and Justice*, noted that the unquestioned ethnocentric profile of the serial killer as a white male in the U.S. was created by the FBI, and subsequent media portrayals have reinforced this myth. Consequently, according to Branson, "The predominant media portrayals of serial murderers are white male perpetrators. The impact of race-based assumptions among law enforcement agencies and the public regarding the criminality of any group poses a danger to that whole society."

Did Bad Henry select his victims because they were Black? "There was no real evidence to verify if this conclusion is true," explained Charisse Coston, an Associate Professor of Criminal Justice and Criminology at the University of North Carolina at Charlotte. "He just knew the victims, and they happened to be black (sic)."

Regardless, Wallace fell from under the law enforcement radar, which enabled him to kill with impunity. Meanwhile, the Hawk and Spain murders remained unsolved, much to the frustration of the victims' loved ones.

FIVE

A Violent Killer

When nothing happened to him after he had killed his first five victims in Charlotte, Wallace's confidence and arrogance grew. Add to this his growing crack cocaine problem, which forced his need for money to support the habit. It was inevitable that Wallace would continue his brutal and violent campaign in Charlotte against young, vulnerable Black women.

It was not the violence of his killings that got Wallace going, according to psychiatric nurse, Dr. Ann Burgess. It was the memory of his crimes. In her book, *Killer by Design,* Burgess writes, "...for Wallace, the act of violence itself wasn't the point. What really thrilled him was playing out these crimes over and over again in his head, refining each recollection until he could recall every last horrific detail. He'd committed his crimes to have memories of them. This was his means of finding and maintaining the emotional connections he failed to create with others." So, Wallace would kill again and again until, hopefully, he was caught.

Wallace never thought he would kill Valencia Jumper, the young, warm, and kind woman he would later describe as being like a sister to him. They had been friends for a little over a year and often spent time together, with Wallace visiting Jumper at her one-bedroom Greenbrye apartment.

Valencia Jumper was born on May 10, 1972, in Columbia, South Carolina, the youngest of five children in a tight family household. Jumper would eventually have two sons herself: Ernee and Nasean. Valencia, like her siblings, was taught basic family values: obey the Golden Rule, work hard, and respect your elders. Valencia attended First Nazareth Baptist Church where she sang with the choir. Teachers at Columbia High School remember Valencia as a "conscientious friendly (sic) and well-reared young lady."

"Valencia was always laughing and upbeat." Robbie Grice, who was Valencia's homeroom teacher during her four years at Columbia High School, told the *State* newspaper, "What I remember about her most was that she was always smiling. She was bright, upbeat, positive (sic) and never cross. She was the kind of student who embodied the ideal—if you work hard and have a good attitude, you'll succeed."

Big things were expected of young Valencia. When she was a senior at Columbia High School in 1990, her parents took out an ad in the yearbook that said: "You've made us proud through the years. Now this is your year to move on to higher heights. We hope and pray that God's grace stays with you while you strive for your goal in life. Best wishes from the both of us. We love you—Mom and Dad."

In an article in the *State* newspaper, dated March 21, 1994, Valencia's high school French teacher recalled how Valencia would speak French to her whenever she went through Valencia's checkout line at the Food Lion on Winnsboro Highway where she worked after her graduation from Colombia High. "She knew it pleased me," Hall told the newspaper. "She is—she was—a young lady who enjoyed pleasing people. She was not selfish, but selfless, always looking out for others."

With dreams, ambitions, and big career plans, Jumper came to Charlotte to attend Johnson C Smith College. She majored in computer science with the goal of working in the computer technology field. To support her education, she worked part-time jobs as a cashier at Food Lion on Charlotte's Central Avenue and as a clerk in the junior department at Hecht's Department Store.

She shared an apartment with a roommate at Greenbryre off Sharon Amity Road, but by the start of her senior year, Valencia's roommate had moved out and she was living alone. On August 9, 1993, Wallace had been walking around the neighborhood and decided to stop by to see Jumper. It was not unusual for Wallace to do this. He would often come over, and he and Valencia would lie on the couch, Wallace on one end and she on the other. Wallace would cook for them and Valencia washed dishes, or vice versa.

Wallace later claimed that he never had any desires to make sexual advances toward Jumper until she lived alone. "I made several passes at her…and there was an occasion where we weren't sexually involved, but we were intimately hugging," Wallace later recalled. "We did have a kiss once or twice, but she felt that it was best that nothing ever came of that because she had a lot of respect for Sadie McKnight (Wallace's girlfriend)."

Jumper trusted Wallace to the point where he had a set of keys to her car, a 1987 red Nissan Sentra. Wallace would go to her house at night and take her Sentra and drive around. He would bring it back and park it in the same spot from which he took the car. She questioned Wallace several times if he was the one who was moving her car. Wallace would lie to her and say no.

The night of August 9, 1993, Jumper woke up from her sleep on the couch and answered the door. It was Henry Wallace. She let him in and they talked about an accident that had occurred at her apartment. The previous April 1, Wallace had used her car and hit a Wells Fargo vehicle. Wallace had agreed to pay the insurance premium on her car. They talked for fifteen to twenty minutes and then Wallace left for home.

Wallace returned to Jumper's apartment about thirty minutes later. Jumper had already taken a shower and had changed into her night clothes. Wallace asked Valencia to call Sadie McKnight, his girlfriend, because they had gotten into a fight. McKnight did not believe where Wallace had been. "Could you please call Sadie and tell her I was here," Wallace asked Jumper.

Wallace later told the police that Sadie McKnight "had always thought Valencia and I had something going because we were really so close, but the fact of the matter was we were like brother and sister."

Jumper agreed to call Sadie. She turned her back and reached for the phone; Wallace made a spur of the moment decision. He decided to kill her. Wallace told police investigators he had just started using cocaine and needed money to buy the drug and that the motive for the murder was a little bit of both sex and robbery. "I had become very attracted to her. But I don't know, somewhere, somehow, once I started doing it, even if the assault was not for money it ended up being for money, I always took something for money, something that could bring me money."

When Jumper let Wallace into the apartment, he had made his mind up about what he was going to do with Jumper. Wallace told psychiatric nurse Ann Burgess, "The attack on Jumper was as soon as I came into the house. Bang, I was on it. I never thought it would happen with Jumper."

He put Jumper in a chokehold and ordered her to move to the bedroom. Terrified, Jumper pleaded with Wallace not to hurt her. "I will do anything you want," Jumper pleaded. She asked Wallace to remove his hands from her throat. She would not scream. She was indeed willing to do anything Wallace asked.

Wallace forced Jumper to remove her clothes and they engaged in oral sex. Jumper started to cry. Wallace asked her why she was crying. She said it was because she had gone through an experience like this in high school. Wallace got scared when she told him that she had told the school about the incident.

They then engaged in sexual intercourse for an hour to an hour and a half. It was a longer time than for any of the other rape victims Wallace had murdered, he later told police. It had been about fifteen minutes for the other victims.

Wallace went to the bathroom and grabbed a towel, which he used to wipe the sweat from his face and body. Wallace returned to Jumper who was putting her clothes back on. As she turned to put her shoes on, Wallace put a towel around her neck and threw her on the bed. He choked her until she passed out. Wallace then continued to choke her until he noticed blood running from her nose and mouth.

Wallace got scared and kept the pressure on the towel for about five minutes until he felt no pulse. He took several rings from her hands, including a half-carat diamond, a smaller carat diamond ring, and a couple of gold rings. He also took her school ring, which he later threw behind the dumpster at the Granville apartments. He pawned the rest of the rings for about one hundred and fifty dollars.

Wallace removed the battery from the smoke detector and then wiped his fingerprints from certain areas of the apartment. He looked for Valencia's purse but could not find it.

Wallace noticed a pint of rum. He took the bottle to the bedroom and poured the rum on Jumper's body, the bed, and the floor. He then went back into the kitchen, opened a can of beans, put the beans in a pot on the stove, and turned the stove on high.

Wallace returned to the bedroom, lit a match, and threw it on Jumper's rum-soaked body. As he went downstairs, he looked up. He could see the curtain and blinds catching fire. He walked away, but about fifteen minutes later had second thoughts and went back to the house.

He didn't see the fire anymore. He thought it had gone out. So he went to the bedroom in an attempt to start another fire. He saw smoke coming from the crack of her door. Figuring the fire was still going, he left. Wallace returned to the apartment twenty minutes later. When he saw smoke rushing out the door, he realized the fire was still going, and he left once again.

Why did Wallace start a fire? He later told police detectives: "I didn't want her murder to seem like the others. I didn't want to continue the chain. I wanted to find a different method."

On August 9, 1993, Zachary Douglas, a friend of Jumper's, spoke with her on the phone about meeting later that night. Subsequently, Douglas arrived at Jumper's apartment in the early morning hours of August 10, 1993 and noticed smoke coming from her apartment. Douglas later testified in court that he had turned the doorknob and found the door unlocked. He opened the door, but found that there was too much smoke for him to enter the apartment. He alerted a neighbor, who called the fire department.

As firefighters arrived on the scene to fight the fire, firefighter Dennis Arney entered the kitchen and noticed that a burner on the stove had been left on. Based on examinations at the fire scene, the information provided by firefighters, and the observed pattern the fire traveled, the investigators believed the fire originated from a pot left burning on the stove. Firefighters found Jumper's body in the bedroom of her apartment.

The next day, Wallace's girlfriend came by to see Wallace at work and informed him that Valencia had died in a fire. Wallace pretended to be in shock and left his job. A few days later, Wallace attended Jumper's funeral with his sister. He even sent the Jumper family condolences. Later, Wallace tried to rationalize the murder to police, "I really don't think that under any normal circumstances would I have ever done that to her because she was like a sister to me."

In August 1993, medical examiner Dr. James Sullivan performed an autopsy on Jumper's extensively charred body. Dr. Sullivan was told that the fire was thought to have been accidentally caused by a pot of beans left burning on the stove. However, he found no soot in Jumper's airway. This indicated to him that there was no significant inhalation of smoke during the fire. When he learned that there was no carbon monoxide in Jumper's blood, Dr. Sullivan listed thermal burns as the cause of death and concluded in the autopsy that Jumper's death was accidental.

Dr. Sullivan, however, had made a big mistake. He wrote in the autopsy report that she had died in the fire. If he would have examined Jumper thoroughly, he would have discovered that she had been strangled before someone had set fire to her lifeless body in order to destroy evidence.

By now, Wallace was on to his next victim. He had known Michelle Stinson, the 20-year-old mother of one- and three-year-old boys, for a long time. She was hard working and aiming for a career in graphic arts. She was doing well at Central Piedmont Community College, making A's and B's in courses like desktop publishing, printing management, sculpture, and water color.

Wallace had met Stinson one day when he was coming to work at Taco Bell. He saw her car stalled in the middle of the street and turned his car around and offered her help. Stinson was pregnant at the time. Wallace got her phone number and they would chat occasionally on the phone. One of Stinson's uncles, with whom Stinson was living at the time, tried to dissuade Wallace from seeing Michelle because he thought she was too young for Wallace to be dating. The uncle ended up advising Wallace that if he had sex with Michelle, he should be sure to use protection.

About six months passed and Wallace had not heard from Michelle. Then one day she ran into Wallace at a McDonald's and recognized him. They exchanged pleasantries and she gave Wallace her new phone number. Wallace eventually called and they had several phone conversations. Wallace was careful. He would always call Stinson from a pay phone. He would never call Stinson from home for fear that the calls could be traced back to him.

Stinson also gave Wallace her address. "I will stop by and see you some time," Wallace told Stinson.

Wallace had a friend drop him off at Stinson's apartment. He had to look around the neighborhood until he found her place. It was about 11 o'clock at night when Stinson opened the door and was surprised to see Wallace. She was a little perturbed that he had not called her first. Wallace said he was just in the area and thought he would drop by. He would not stay long. He just wanted to talk with someone. Stinson let Wallace into the house.

Stinson put her one-year-old son to bed and they chatted briefly. Wallace asked Stinson for a glass of water. She got it for him. He drank the water, gave the glass back to her, and said he had to leave. Take care. Stinson put the glass in the sink and they hugged.

But Wallace knew what he was going to do to Stinson. He was determined that he was going to rape and kill her. Later Wallace recalled to police investigators. "She was very vulnerable. I knew she would be easy, so to speak."

Wallace told Stinson that he wanted to have sex with her. Take off your clothes, he ordered. Stinson got scared and told Wallace that she was sick. Wallace believed she was lying and he demanded that she prove it to him. Stinson said she couldn't. "Well do you have any medication for it," Wallace asked. Stinson said no.

Wallace grabbed Stinson and proceeded to choke her. Stinson pleaded that Wallace stop. She would have sex with him. She took her clothes off. Wallace said he was going to have oral sex with her, but she said she did not how to do it. Wallace said: "Well I guess you got to learn."

Stinson did oral sex on Wallace and he got an erection. He pulled her down to the kitchen floor and they had sex. After Wallace was done, he applied the chokehold on Stinson until she passed out. Wallace then went to the bathroom, got a towel, returned to Stinson, and proceeded to coldly strangle her to death. Wallace thought she was dead, but she continued to moan and groan. Wallace went to the kitchen, got a knife, returned to Stinson, and stabbed her four times as she gasped for breath. All this happened while Stinson's two sons were sleeping in their beds.

Wallace looked at the body and could see the blood dripping from her nose and mouth. He put a towel across her head in case the sons woke up, came out into the kitchen, and saw their mother. They would not see the blood. Wallace used a washcloth to wipe his fingerprints from the glass, the door, the phone, the wall, and the floor.

Before Wallace left the apartment, Stinson's oldest son awoke. Wallace told him to go back to bed. Concluding that Stinson had nothing of value to steal, he made no effort to rob her. He left her place and threw the knife and washcloth over a fence near the back of Stinson's apartment.

On September 15, 1993, Stinson's friend, James Mayes, stopped by Stinson's apartment to see her. Mayes knocked on the front door, but no one answered. He heard the children knocking on the window and telling him their mother was sleeping on the kitchen floor. He thought the Stinson family was playing a game.

Mayes turned to leave when the oldest child came out the back door and grabbed him. Mayes picked up the child and went back into the apartment through the back door. Mayes discovered Stinson lying on the kitchen floor with blood around her. Mayes picked up the phone but realized the cord had been cut or jerked out of the wall. Mayes took the children and hurried to the neighbors where he asked them to help him find a phone to call the police.

The police arrived at Stinson's home. "I will always remember the Stinson case," recalled Garry McFadden, who headed the Wallace investigation. "When our officers arrived, Michelle's boys were calmly watching television, and their mother was dead on the floor."

Dr. James Sullivan performed an autopsy on Stinson's body on September 16, 1993. He concluded that the cause of Stinson's death was stab wounds to the chest with strangulation as a contributing cause. He discovered four stab wounds to the left side of the back. Two of the four stab wounds caused injury to the heart and lungs and were potentially fatal. Dr. Sullivan also observed evidence of ligature strangulation in the form of a band of abrasions and contusions over the front of the neck and small hemorrhages in the skin of the face, the conjunctiva, and internally in the muscles of Stinson's neck. This time the strangling occurred after Stinson had suffered the knife wounds and while she lay dying and comatose.

The police questioned family, friends, and associates of the dead women, but were still not making any connections. Each of Wallace's murder victims were being investigated individually by a different police investigator, and no effort was being made on behalf of the investigators to compare notes. In some of the cases, the police missed the obvious. For example, it was common knowledge that Michelle Stinson was known to be a friend of Henry Wallace and that she ate frequently at the Taco Bell where Wallace worked. Still no connection was made between them despite the fact that there had been five deaths/disappearances in fifteen months, all within a five-mile radius inside East Charlotte.

Meanwhile, many in the close-knit East Charlotte community were getting frustrated with what appeared to be the police's indifference to the killings and their lack of progress in the cases. As the killings mounted, they began to suspect that racism may have been involved. After all, the victims were young women, poor, and Black. There were few news headlines or news trucks covering the cases and their murders went largely unnoticed.

As the Colombia, South Carolina, *State* newspaper reported on March 16, 1994, "The mourning of family and friends were virtually unnoticed in this city of 417,621 people. Motherless children were absorbed into other families without a sound. The list of sisters lost quietly grew longer. And all the while a killer was free."

The *Charlotte Observer*, however, investigated the charge of racism and in a report published March 21, 1994, concluded that the facts didn't support the racism charge. Among other findings, the breakdown by race of Black females for unsolved murders in 1993 found 35 percent unsolved, Black males, 22 percent unsolved, white females, 20 percent unsolved, and white males, 60 percent unsolved. Further statistics for unsolved rapes broken down by race in 1993 indicated Black females, 52 percent unsolved, white females, 54 percent unsolved. The newspaper concluded: "In the end the facts about this case will speak for themselves. But those known so far don't establish a pattern of racist neglect."

The Charlotte police asked the FBI for assistance, but the FBI said that the murders were not the work of a serial killer. According to FBI serial murder profiler Robert, who later testified at Wallace's trial: "If he elected to become a serial killer, he was going about it the wrong way. Mr. Wallace always seemed to take one step forward and two steps back. He would take items and put them in the stove to destroy them by burning them and then forget to turn the stove on."

On February 4, 1994, Wallace was arrested for shoplifting from an area mall within walking distance of most of the murder sites. He was booked on shoplifting charges, given a court date, and released. Wallace, however, failed to show up for his court date. There is no evidence that the authorities tried to arrest and charge Wallace for failure to appear in court. A computer check might have revealed his lengthy police record, which included burglary convictions and sexual assault charges in two states. If they had, they might have caught on to Wallace being the Taco Bell killer and lives would have been saved.

By now, Wallace must have concluded that he had little to fear from the authorities. They had arrested him, but had let him go. They even had a warrant for his arrest, but there is no indication that they made an effort to find and arrest him.

As it was, sixteen days later he would kill again, then again, and again.

SIX

Kill Zone

The predominantly Black population of East Charlotte was frightened and angry. Young Blacks were being murdered and the Charlotte Metropolitan Police Department (CMPD) had no real leads on the killer. There had been five deaths of young African American women within a five-mile radius of East Charlotte. Charlotte's Black community wanted answers.

Under pressure, the CMPD knew it had to do something. So, the police department held a news conference to make a couple of important announcements. First, it would increase patrols in East Charlotte. Secondly, it appointed veteran police officer Sergeant Garry McFadden, an African American, to head the investigation into the murders.

McFadden was born in Sumpter, South Carolina, but grew up in Elliott, South Carolina, a small, tight-knit community of about 300 people, located about two hours from Charlotte, east of Colombia off of Interstate 20. He was an aggressive and talkative kid. "We grew up knowing and liking our neighborhood," McFadden recalled. "A lot of young people who have come from Elliott have done quite well for themselves."

He arrived in Charlotte in 1978 to attend Johnson C. Smith University. Three years later, he graduated with a degree in physical education. After college, he wanted to be a football coach, but, on impulse, he applied to be police officer with the Charlotte Metropolitan Police Department (CMPD).

He was one of several Black applicants but was rejected. "They rejected four of us, and to this day I don't know why," McFadden revealed. "I didn't take the rejection well, but I persevered, applied again (sic) and was hired. All of us who were rejected went on to have great careers in law enforcement."

McFadden spent the first three years as a patrol officer, policing West Boulevard and the public housing communities of Southside Homes and Dalton Village. McFadden gained valuable experience in how to deal with the community." In working the streets, I learned to communicate with people," McFadden explained. "We in law enforcement have not done well dealing with the community and building bridges. Today, I can go to the communities and interact with people, and I am welcome."

McFadden became a detective in 1985 and focused on investigating burglaries. After a stint on the armed robbery task force, he joined the homicide squad and spent twenty-two years with it.

McFadden is charismatic and his gift of gab became a key part of his police work. He told the *Charlotte Observer* on August 7, 2011, "My style is totally candid. I talk to people all the time. And my approach is non-police style. I will start a conversation with you just about your shoes you got on or make a joke or something. I don't knock on the door, and say, "I'm the police and flip my badge. Then they're on the defense already."

Some cynics in the Charlotte community scoffed at McFadden's appointment to head the investigation of young Black women murders, claiming that he had been put in the position because he was Black. Glenn Counts, a reporter at the time at WCNC, the television station in Charlotte, disagreed with that claim. "To be honest, there are (crime) situations involving African Americans where you definitely want an African American in place," Counts explained. "That's not to say that Garry (McFadden) isn't a very capable investigator. He is one of the best to work in the (CMPD) homicide unit. He's qualified to get the job done."

McFadden provides a blunt response to the question: Was he appointed to head the Wallace investigation because he was African American? "The CMPD needed someone to take the blame if the Wallace investigation went bad," McFadden said. "I am African American, so that worked out nicely for them. No one can tell me differently. But I went out into the community and heard the complaints. I never ran from them (the community)."

McFadden would rise to prominence in the CMPD and eventually starred in a documentary series, *I Am Homicide*, on the Investigation Discovery Channel. In 2011, he retired and was promptly rehired to work with the police chief's office. By the time he ran for sheriff in 2022 and won the election, he had become a local celebrity.

But back in 1993, when McFadden was assigned to the Wallace murder case, he faced a formidable mother of one of the victims. Dee Sumpter, the mother of Shawna Hawk, was dissatisfied with the way the murder investigation of her daughter was moving. At the time, the CMPD was going through what Sumpter describes as "monumental change. The CMPD was in shambles," she recalled. "They had an acting chief of police who I don't think was up to the job. I became a pariah to the police. They tried to ignore me, but I wouldn't allow it."

Sumpter recalled when one homicide detective working the case called her and promised that he would be in touch with her to let her know where the CMPD was with the investigation. "To this day, he has not called me," Sumpter revealed. "He knows where I work, where I live."

When McFadden took charge of the investigation, he thought it would be better to form an alliance with Sumpter than to ignore her. Sumpter was invited by the CMPD to give "sensitivity training" to the rank and file. But Sumpter was only allowed to give one session, a situation she describes as "a band aid on a gaping wound….(sic)They (the police) listened and were cordial," Sumpter recalled. "I taught them that if they wanted to be successful in their job, it behooved them to get to know the communities they patrolled and not just show up when a robbery, murder, domestic violence incident (sic) or whatever occurred. Be visible in the community and get to know the people who live there. So that when you arrive, you are met with respect and have a communication line established."

Sumpter added that they needed to forget the script of what they were taught in the police academy. "The police need to go off script and put themselves in the position of the citizen," she explained.

When McFadden took over the investigation, Sumpter let him know what she thought of the way it was going. "From day one, I told Garry I was not happy," Sumpter revealed. "I was not pleased. 'Your department has lied to me. Why can't the dots (in the case) be connected? A reporter sitting in a fricking news room (sic) is doing your job. What is the problem? Can you answer that, Mr. McFadden? I want answers, to have somebody arrested. I want you to do your job and find out who is killing these women.'"

McFadden listened to Sumpter's candid comments, and the police approach to the murder investigation began to change. The CMPD began to keep Sumpter in the loop, contacting her every few days to let her know what was going on. "It encouraged me," Sumpter said.

McFadden credits Sumpter with keeping the public's attention on her daughter's murder. "There was a man who stepped forward and offered a $10,000 reward for information leading to the identification of Dee's daughter's killer," McFadden recalled. "He put the money in a John Hancock Mutual Fund anonymously. We didn't know anything about him. We were never able to identify him, but we didn't take the money."

In February 1994, twenty-five-year-old Vanessa Little Mack, a graduate of North Mecklenburg High and Gainesville (Florida) Business College, was working as a Carolina Medical Center patients' escort. She had two daughters, Natara and Natalia, aged seven and four months. Those who knew Vanessa describe her as beautiful, smart, and bright-eyed. Colleagues at the Carolina Medical Center remember her as a hard-working person who showed concern for the patients.

Wallace knew Mack for some time and had dated Vanessa's sister, Leslie Little, who had worked with Wallace at the Taco Bell on Sharon Amity Road and with two of Wallace's previous victims. Wallace was an Assistant Manager at the Taco Bell.

Wallace invited Little to lunch at a pizza parlor on Freedom Drive. Little had a good time. Little told Wallace her problems and he offered a sympathetic ear. On a second date in July 1993, Little invited her sister, Vanessa Little Mack, to come. Vanessa did come, and Wallace told Leslie Little that he liked her sister.

Mack confided to Wallace about her problems with her boyfriend and he would give her advice. Wallace became like a brother to Mack. He would pick up her baby from daycare and even take her wherever she wanted to go.

"I stalked her (Vanessa Mack) for several months," Wallace told forensic nurse, Ann Burgess. "I had fantasies of having rough sex with her. She was a very attractive woman. We went out a few times. But then rejection came. She didn't like the dinners. She led me to believe we'd be more than friends."

Mack became pregnant by someone else and she moved. Wallace lost contact with her. One day, he was driving his

1987 Cutlass Sierra Oldsmobile and spotted Mack at a bus stop. Wallace gave her a ride to her new residence at 2945 Greenland Avenue. Mack gave Wallace her phone number and told him to call her.

Wallace explained later to police investigators: "At first I was a little disappointed because I never had the relationship that I wanted with her, as I really just wanted to be her friend, you know, just kind of continue in that manner."

Mack's baby was about to be born the same time Wallace was to have his baby. Three weeks after Mack had her baby, Wallace paid Mack a visit. He had gone by several times before, but she never answered the door.

Wallace's crack habit was getting worse and he needed money to support his habit. Wallace later admitted that he had every intention of robbing and murdering Mack. Wallace wanted to be sure she was home, so he called her, and when she answered, he hung up. When Wallace arrived at her apartment, he made another phone call to Mack. She answered Wallace's call. Wallace hung up again. He now knew she was home.

Wallace then walked up to her apartment and knocked on the door. Mack did not answer. He went back to the pay phone and called Vanessa again. She answered.

Wallace asked: "Why don't you answer your door?"

"Is that Henry?" she responded.

Wallace replied, "Yeah."

Mack told Wallace she would let him in the back door. He said he would be there in a couple of minutes. After letting Wallace in, they chatted for a while, especially about Mack's youngest daughter. Mack admonished Wallace for not coming by more often. Wallace told her she needed to get some security because she was a female living alone. Mack said she might do that now that she got her tax return back. It was for a sum of two thousand dollars. All the while, as they chatted, Wallace was trying to figure out how he could get her in a position so he could strangle her.

He asked Mack for a hug, but she rejected him, saying she was still mad at him for not coming by sooner. Wallace had been there for approximately an hour and a half still trying to figure out how he could get Mack in a position to kill her.

"I'm going to leave," Wallace told Mack. "How about something to drink before I do?" Mack went to the refrigerator and came back with a bottle of Mountain Dew.

Mack turned her back on Wallace, and he pulled out a pillowcase that was tucked inside his shirt. He quickly wrapped it around her neck and applied enough pressure so that she must have known Wallace was trying to kill her. Mack fell down to her knees, terrified. Wallace said, "I'm not joking. This is a robbery (sic)"

Wallace dragged Mack to the bedroom where he demanded to know how much money she had. Mack pulled the money from her purse and handed it to Wallace.

"How much money do you have in your bank account?" Wallace demanded.

Mack told him that she only had three hundred dollars in her bank account.

Wallace said, "You just told me you got $2,000 back in income tax." Then he demanded she give him her bank teller card. Quivering in fear, she handed it over to Wallace.

"What's your pin number," Wallace demanded, and she gave him her pin number.

Wallace then ordered Mack to remove her bra and panties. Mack asked Wallace if he could remove the towel from around her neck. She would not scream, Mack assured Wallace. Wallace loosened the towel from around Mack's neck but didn't remove it.

Wallace then had sex with Mack for approximately half an hour. When he finished, Wallace ordered Mack to put her clothes back on. After she had done that, Wallace tightened the towel around Mack's neck until she passed out. He put a blanket and pillow on top of her face and proceeded to wipe down the place for fingerprints and other evidence. Wallace checked on the baby, staying with her until she went to sleep. When he left Mack's place, he kept the back door open.

"It was easier for me to take Vanessa's life and not really give a whole lot of concern about her child because I knew— she had told me—that the lady next door always kept an eye on her," Wallace later told investigators. "I knew that if the baby started crying, (sic) and Vanessa didn't respond, then the lady next door would come over. That's why I left the back door open. I left the back door cracked so the lady could easily come in."

Wallace hurried down the street to a nearby service station and called a cab. He threw the pillowcase that he had used on Mack in a dumpster behind the store, then caught the cab. He also tore up Mack's checkbook that he had taken from the house. When he got back to the east side of town, he found a teller machine and tried to withdraw money using Mack's bank card. It didn't work. Wallace tried to use the card at three different banks, but they all failed. Mack had given Wallace a phony pin number. He knew cameras were at the teller machines, so he approached them with his head down so as not to be identified.

On Sunday morning, February 20, 1994, Barbara Rippy, the grandmother of Mack's oldest daughter, went to Mack's apartment to pick up Mack's youngest daughter, as she did every Sunday. She did it so Mack could go to work. Mack had a troubled childhood and she did not always show patience with her daughters, but she was trying to do better. Rippy told the *Charlotte Observer*, "I was a mother to her…I use (sic) to tell her to watch whom she associated with. We had our times. I'll tell you that."

Rippy arrived at 6:00 a.m. and went to the back door, but the door was ajar. As she entered, Rippy noticed Mack's four-month-old daughter lying on the couch, which she thought was an unusual thing for Vanessa to allow. Rippy called out to Vanessa, but Mack did not respond.

Rippy made her way through the house and entered the bedroom. She saw Mack's feet hanging off the side of the bed. Rippy later testified that Mack's feet were the only part of her body exposed and that they appeared gray and felt cold. Something was wrapped around her throat. It looked like a pillowcase. Next to Mack lay her purse, its contents strewn on the bed. Rippy called to Mack to get up, but she did not move. When she turned on the bedroom light and saw Mack, to her horror she realized that she was dead. Mack had been strangled to death.

Rippy picked up Mack's daughter, dashed into the hallway, and pounded on a tenant's door to use their phone to call 9-1-1.

Fire department and police department vehicles arrived. Officer Jeffrey Baumgardner of the Charlotte-Mecklenburg Police Department was the first patrolman on the scene. He found Mack lying on her bed. Bumgardner also noticed a pocketbook, with its contents scattered on the bed. He observed a towel combined with a long-sleeve shirt around Mack's neck and blood coming from her nose, ears, face, and the muscles in the front of the neck. He also observed small areas of bruising beneath the ligature, likely caused by the pinching of the ligature. The killing was brutal. One detective noted that "it was the most extreme case I've seen."

Police noticed that there was no forced entry, nor was anything disturbed in the house. The police officers figured that the victim most likely knew her killer. The purse was on the bed, its contents strewn, suggesting that robbery might have been the motive. The police learned that her bank card was missing. They went looking at nearby ATM locations, hoping to get a photo identifying a possible assailant. The police saw a Black male with a gold earring using Mack's card. But the photo is grainy and not clear enough to identify the man.

Dr. James M. Sullivan performed an autopsy on Mack's body on February 21, 1994. He observed minimal evidence of blunt trauma as well as evidence of strangulation. There was a ligature in place around Mack's neck. The ligature was made of a long-sleeve pullover type shirt and a towel. Dr. Sullivan also observed small hemorrhages in the conjunctiva and on the skin. The cause of Mack's death, Sullivan determined, was strangulation.

Wallace returned to his apartment that night, empty handed. She had lied to him about her bank account pin. He admonished himself for being so naïve as to accept Mack's word. He thought about Mack's murder and felt some remorse. He did like her. She was a nice girl who liked him and treated him well. Why did he do it?

He had gone to see Mack to get the money he needed for his next fix. He was desperate, out of crack, and he had no money to buy the drug. He remembered the nosy neighbor at Mack's house. Did he hear anything about what was going on at Mack's apartment? He decided to be safe and stay out of sight.

The night of the murder, Wallace plopped himself on the couch, got the remote and turned on the television. Surely there would be some report about what happened at the Mack apartment. The news came on, and when it finished, Wallace shrugged and smiled. Not a word, nothing about the strangling of his latest victim, nothing, in fact, about the investigation into the murders of young Black women the police claimed they were pursuing diligently.

Yet, there were clues in the autopsies conducted by Dr. Sullivan that were red flags and could have pointed the police investigators to the fact that the murders were committed by one killer. Valencia Jumper had died in a fire, but the conclusion was wrong. She was strangled. Both Shawna Hawk and Aubrey Spain were strangled, and there were obvious signs of strangulation in Michelle Stinson's death.

WSOC TV in Charlotte in its investigation titled "Body of Evidence: The Wallace Investigation" interviewed Vernon Geberth, a retired lieutenant commander of the New York City Police Department with over forty years' experience in police work. Geberth told WSOC that the CMPD missed an obvious serial pattern and that this pattern should have been recognized in 1993, early in their investigation.

Yet the CMPD saw no similarities, no distinctive characteristics to determine the three murders were connected. Dr. James Sullivan said that "he relied on the fire investigators for the information he needed to complete his autopsy on Valencia Jumper.

David Coverly, chief fire investigator in the Jumper murder investigation, tried to explain to WSOC how the fire investigators reached their conclusion. "Super heated (sic) air can kill someone without leaving traces of carbon monoxide in the lungs or the throat," he explained. "I've seen this often."

Coverly's conclusion was also questioned in the WSOC television segment by Dr. Cyril Wecht, American forensic pathologist. Dr. Wecht said he had a problem with the investigation. "I don't want to sound too harsh," Dr. Wecht explained. "I find the explanation unscientific and invalid as applied to this particular (Wallace) case." According to Wecht, superheated air is found in blast furnaces and large chemical explosions, not apartment fires, so he could not come to the same conclusion as Coverly.

The CMPD homicide division may have been under pressure and criticism, but under Garry McFadden's leadership, it was working diligently behind the scenes to connect the dots in the murder investigation. It investigated suspects with violent pasts, contrary to Dee Sumpter's claims about the police effort that it had neglected to talk to people who knew the victims. The CMPD claimed its detectives were keeping in contact with family and friends of the victims, as they looked for a thread running through the case histories. Did they have the same friends? Did they work together? Did they frequent the same places?

According to McFadden those questions were being asked. Still, remarkably, the investigation was missing important details. For instance, it did not note that Mack's sister worked at the same Taco Bell as Shawna Hawk or Audrey Spain.

In the East Charlotte community, word was spreading that young Black women were being murdered. It sent a chill through the community. "I knew people in the community who were really concerned," Counts recalls. "My girl-friend (sic) at the time lived on that side of Charlotte where Wallace was killing. I told her to be careful and not to let people she didn't know into her place."

The problem was that Wallace did not fit the profile of the typical serial killer. First, he was a Black man. The typical serial killer is invariably thought to be white. Second, a typical serial killer takes the lives of strangers, but in all of his murders Wallace knew the victims.

So, in escaping the serial killer profile, Henry Wallace had been lucky, even though he had been sloppy, even reckless, in his murderous rampage. As his drug habit got worse, he was abandoning the precautions that he had taken previously to cover for himself: spacing out the murders, wiping clean the crime scene, even bathing some of the victims. But the evidence indicated that his addiction was now out of control. He did not get any money from his last victim, Vanessa Mack, and he was too broke to get a fix. He was desperate. And his life was falling apart.

Wallace had lost his job at the Black Eye Pea Restaurant. In February 1994, girlfriend Sadie McKnight threw Wallace out after she discovered he had been using crack. She reportedly filed reports with the police, complaining he had pushed her around and taken money for drugs. They also argued over the other woman, Wanda Harrison, who had had Wallace's baby.

Wallace phoned McKnight and begged her to take him back, but she refused. After the call, Wallace stood holding the phone, crying. The split with McKnight left Wallace very upset. "I asked her to try to understand what the addiction was like, and she stood by me for a little while, but she left me when I really needed her the most," Wallace later recalled for police investigators. "I am not blaming her for my actions because it started way before her, but the things that were going on within the last week, if she was just there when I needed somebody, these other three women (Baucom, Henderson (sic) and Slaughter) would not be dead."

Wallace added: "I was homeless. I didn't have a job. The addiction had taken over me to the effect where I couldn't even sleep even if I wasn't doing the drug. I couldn't think straight."

To relieve his anxiety, Wallace would walk and walk. "I just started walking around and around and around, and I walked so much that day (when McKnight kicked him out) that that's when my feet started getting sore in my shoes. My muscles in here (in my feet) started locking up, and I couldn't stop walking. I mean, I wanted to just sit down."

Friends reported that Wallace had sold everything in his apartment, including the weights that helped build up his impressive 6'1", 240-pound frame.

Once neat and tidy, he stopped changing his clothes, shaved his head, and lost weight. Wallace tried to keep up appearances, remaining calm and polite, especially with females, but he looked strung out, like he was experiencing some life-changing trauma.

If you listen to Wallace, he was feeling some remorse at what he had done and was doing. Later, Wallace would try to explain himself to the law. "I know that I'm sick," he told his CMPD interrogators. "No one ever in this room has said to me, I don't understand. I know you don't understand, but even with something this serious, people in other cases when it was minor, the first thing that would come out of their mouth is, I don't understand. They never tried. They never tried to listen. People would like to hear what you have to say, but there's a big difference between hearing and listening., (sic) and all I ever wanted for somebody to do was just listen to the cries that I had, the reasoning behind it, because there's always a message."

Larry Spencer, who lived near Wallace, recalled for the *Charlotte Observer* how Wallace had come over to his place and called the Greyhound Bus Depot to see what time the bus was leaving for Barnwell. He said he needed to get away, get his head together. He wanted to visit his mom. Spencer offered Wallace a ride to the bus station. Wallace profusely thanked Spencer and complained that "everybody else had turned their back on him."

Wallace never did take that bus. He should have. The police were about to make some discoveries that would put him in their cross hairs.

SEVEN

The Screw Up

On March 9, 1994, Henry Wallace was feeling cocky. He had been on a murderous roll, rampaging in East Charlotte, North Carolina, and the cops were clueless. Wallace had constantly watched the TV evening news for information that the police were on to him, but they still hadn't connected the dots. He smiled as he watched outraged Black citizens complain about the lack of action on the part of the police in solving the murders. They demanded to know: Was the lack of action because all seven victims were Black?

Wallace was abusing drugs but he had the good sense to keep a low profile and out of sight just in case someone might have spotted him at the scene of one of his crimes. Or, maybe, the police had a composite drawing of him and were on the street looking for him. He didn't feel too good about the murders. He never did. But he knew that feeling would go away.

The Charlotte police conceded that they were stumped by the killings. And why shouldn't they have been? After all, each case was being handled by a different police investigator. No notes were compared and no links made. The police treated each of the murders separately.

Wallace didn't fit the mold of a typical serial killer either. He looked normal. Around six feet in height, a little overweight, low key, disarming manner, Wallace could get lost in a crowd. He was slick, with a solicitous attitude, and women were taken in by his charm. He knew all of his victims and was able to gain the trust of each and every one of them.

Then there was Wallace's nagging craving for drugs. Wallace recalled for police investigators the one night he bought a quarter ounce of cocaine from a drug dealer named Eddy. "I smoked it all in one day. I passed out many times…I just started having nervous twitches. I would pass out and I would come back, though, and I would just take another hit. I wasn't concerned about living. I guess at that point, that's when I realized I really wanted to die because I was fucking up too bad."

So, while smug in his belief that he was gaming the system, his vision of reality was being distorted by his mental condition and his drug hit. And being in desperate straits, with his crack cocaine habit out of control, he didn't have the money for his next fix, and he needed it bad.

He had learned that Vanessa Mack, a co-worker from Taco Bell, a popular fast-food restaurant, had received her income tax check from the IRS. "Vanessa was a vibrant young woman with a great future ahead of her that was, unfortunately, cut short," recalled Garry McFadden, who at the time was a sergeant with the CMPD, and would later head the investigation of the Henry Wallace case. "She lived in what was thought of as being the safe part of Charlotte."

Wallace had seen Mack's ATM card, which she carried around with her. Surely, she would have some money in her bank account, Wallace surmised. He decided to find out for himself.

Wallace had totaled his green Maxima, so he caught a cab to Mack's apartment, on Greenland Avenue where he charmed his way in and then quickly wrapped a pillowcase around her neck, squeezed hard, and demanded she give him her ATM pin number. Even though she complied, Wallace strangled her, then dashed out of the apartment with her ATM card.

He caught a cab and headed for Mack's bank, Bank of America, where he tried using Mack's ATM card, but it didn't work. Mack had given Wallace a fake pin number. Enraged, Wallace pounded the ATM. He was in a sweat, desperate for a fix. He thought for a moment, hailed a cab, and headed off into the night.

In March 1994, Verness Lamar "Squeaky" Woods was living in the Lake apartments (today called the Sailboat Bay apartments) in East Charlotte, right near the Eastland Mall, with his girlfriend, 18-year-old Brandi Henderson, and their ten-month-old son, Tyrese.

Wallace went to the apartments, thinking his friend Woods would be at work, and he would be able to force Henderson to give him the money he needed for his next fix. Desperate for cash and hooked on crack, Wallace planned to rob, rape, and murder the sweet Brandi Henderson.

On March 9, 1994, the day Wallace went to Woods apartment, Woods was at the apartment taking care of Tyrese because Henderson had a doctor's appointment. Woods, lanky and athletic, and Wallace would hang out often in their free time, drinking beer and hitting on young ladies. Wallace and Woods had worked together at Chucky Cheese, and earlier at the Golden Corral.

Brandi Henderson had dropped out of high school, but went back to Harding High to try and get her diploma. She also studied at Central Piedmont Community College. The young girl's life had been tough. Her parents had separated when she was two and she had spent a lot of her life moving from house to house.

Her friends remembered her as always having a positive attitude and wanting to believe the best about people. "She was full of life," Joann Hite, the victim's cousin, recalled in 2007 for the Internet forum, Tapatalk. "She was friendly with everybody. She loved people." Henderson had worked with Woods and Wallace at the Golden Corral.

Wallace rapped on the door of Wood's apartment and was surprised to see

Woods answer.

"Hey brotha, whatcha doin' here?" Woods asked.

"Ah, ah, man…Well, I'm heading out of town," Wallace replied, flustered and lying.

"Heading out of a town?"

"Yeah… yeah, brotha, I thought I would say good bye (sic)."

Looking puzzled, Woods smiled. "Oh, okay. Yeah, man."

"Ah, where's Brandi?" Wallace asked.

"At the doc's," Woods replied. "She'll be back soon. Look, I got to go to work. I'm running a little late."

Wallace and Woods clasped hands and hugged.

Woods said, "You take care, man. Let me know how it goes."

"Yeah, man," Wallace said.

Wallace turned around and walked away. He heard the door to Woods' apartment close. What was he going to do? No money, no fix. But as Wallace left the apartment complex, he stopped. He remembered that he knew someone else at the apartment complex—24-year-old Betty Baucom, who lived with her adopted daughter. Her family affectionately called Betty "Suzie," and friends remember her as beautiful, vivacious, and sweet. She worked as an assistant manager with Wallace's girlfriend, Sadie McKnight, at Bojangles restaurant on Central Avenue. Baucom had talked about transferring to a new Bojangles in Sanford, North Carolina, so she could be closer to her fiancé, but nothing definite had been arranged. Wallace figured surely, Baucom would have the combination to the safe at Bojangles.

Wallace did not know exactly where Baucom lived, but he thought he knew where the neighborhood was. He had the cab drop him off and he began walking. Wallace saw Baucom's car, a bronze colored 1988 Nissan Pulsar, and guessed that she had to live near the car in the apartment complex at the end of the block. He entered the complex and checked some stuff stacked outside the bottom apartment. He figured it was not Baucom's. Maybe it was the apartment above. He went upstairs and rang the doorbell.

He heard, "Who is it?" It was Betty Baucom.

Wallace replied, "Ah, this is Henry Wallace. I need to use your phone."

Baucom knew that Wallace was Brandi Henderson's boyfriend's friend. He was nice and polite. She was more than happy to let Wallace use the phone.

"I played around for a couple of minutes like I had to use her phone," Wallace later recalled for police investigators. "As I was getting ready to leave, I administered the choke hold to Betty… that is where I incurred all these scratches, a bite mark here."

Baucom fell to the ground. Wallace demanded that she give him the alarm code and Bojangles' safe code. Terrified, Baucom agreed to give Wallace everything he wanted.

"Please don't hurt me," she begged. "I won't tell. If you wait until tomorrow, I'll just give you the money and say that I was robbed."

"Nah, I'm not going to do that," Wallace told her.

Baucom then tried to get Wallace to go to the bank with her, but he didn't want to do that either.

Wallace and Baucom then scuffled. That's when Wallace sustained a bite on his shoulder and scratches on his abdomen. Baucom was a fighter. "It was a real struggle," Wallace told police investigators. "She put up a real big fight. I mean, we fought for about twenty minutes before I could even subdue her."

Baucom grabbed Wallace's penis and started pulling. Wallace got control of Baucom and told her to remove her clothes. He wanted her to perform oral sex on him. Baucom told Wallace she did not want to remove her clothes because she had a medical problem. Baucom then showed Wallace a rash she had on her buttocks, which he later told police investigators looked like an ordinary rash. She explained it was the reason she and her boyfriend were having problems.

"Henry, you don't really want to do this to me," Baucom said. "I thought you were a nice guy."

Wallace smirked and replied, "I am a nice guy but I'm very sick. I spent over two thousand dollars in two weeks on cocaine."

Then according to the police interrogation, Wallace told her how he had got the money: "When Sadie became manager (of the Bojangles on Central Avenue), they gave her the combination to the safe in the store. I guess they weren't supposed to write it down. But one day I was just plundering through her work pockets to make sure she didn't have any money or anything (and)... I found the combination to the safe in their store. When she went to sleep one night, I took the keys to the store and went in. I opened the safe, and I took all the money, all the paper money, and the quarters from the safe, and I left and locked the door behind me. I never told her that I did it."

Wallace said he got about $2,100 from the theft. He admitted he did it a second time. "One particular night I saw her put that slip of paper she had the combination written down in a section of her purse, in her wallet, and went to sleep. I got the combination again. I wrote it down on a slip of paper and put that piece of paper back in her pocketbook (sic), just like I found it. But this time, she didn't have the keys, so I had to find a way to get into the store. I took a brick, a rock, and I busted the side door out and went in. It took forever to open that safe. I kept running out to see if anybody was coming. It took me about an hour to get into the safe that time, but I was so desperate for those drugs I had to do it."

The haul was about twenty-eight hundred to three thousand dollars. It was spent on cocaine and gone in under two weeks.

Wallace was persistent in getting Baucom to do what he wanted her to do. He got her to remove her clothes and engage in sexual intercourse with him. After they were finished, Wallace told Baucom to put her clothes back on. He then placed a towel around her neck and asked her if she had any money.

Gasping and crying, Baucom felt her neck. "Why are you doing this to me?" she asked.

Wallace mumbled, "I'm sick. I've hurt many people."

Baucom struggled to stand. "I forgive you. You need help."

Baucom's comment triggered Wallace. He went ballistic and grabbed Baucom by the throat, throwing her to the floor. Baucom screamed and whimpered. They scuffled on the floor. Baucom scratched Wallace.

Wallace told Baucom that he was doing a robbery and demanded the alarm code, keys, and combination to the safe for the Bojangles' restaurant where Baucom was the manager, or he would kill her. Baucom was upset at the trauma of Wallace's vicious attack, but she resisted for nearly thirty minutes.

Baucom grabbed a drinking glass near her bed, filled with water, and hit Wallace on the top of the head, making him a little dizzy. He maneuvered to get behind Baucom and was able to administer pressure on her with the chokehold, rendering her unconscious.

Wallace got increasingly angry. Baucom revived and, finally, she surrendered the information. Wallace then put a towel around Baucom's neck and asked her if she had any money.

"Empty your wallet," Wallace demanded.

"I don't have any money," Baucom insisted.

"Well, open it up and let me see," Wallace ordered.

She gave him the money in her purse, about eighty dollars. Wallace was disappointed at the amount. Wallace then choked her until she was almost unconscious. He took off her clothes and violently raped her.

Afterward, Wallace told Baucom to get dressed. Wallace calmly watched Baucom dress and then proceeded to strangle her to death.

Wallace unclipped the gold chain from around Baucom's neck and pocketed it. He took a wet cloth and wiped the walls, the knobs in the kitchen and bathroom, the phone he had touched, and the wall near where they had been scuffling.

Wallace no longer owned a car. He had totaled his green Maxima, so he took Baucom's Pulsar to transport the stolen items. He packed her TV into the trunk. He had to climb across the passenger seat in order to get into the car because her other door would not open. He drove back to his apartment where he called the man named Larry and told him he was bringing over a TV to sell. He got $50 for it. Later, he used the money to buy crack.

The next day, Wallace brazenly returned to Baucom's apartment, worried that he had left a person for dead who was not dead. But Baucom was dead and her face had turned color to prove it. Satisfied, Wallace took her VCR and left Baucom's apartment.

It was early in the morning and it had started to rain. People had yet to begin the day. As Wallace carried the TV out, he spotted a maintenance man, who looked directly at him. Wallace tensed up, but the maintenance man did not pay further attention to him. The downstairs neighbor came out of the apartment as well and glanced at Wallace, but he did not seem to have any further interest.

Then there was the policeman who walked by and looked directly at him. He did not stop Wallace and ask him what he was doing there. Wallace was becoming paranoid and a nervous wreck. He knew he had to get out of Charlotte real soon.

Wallace breathed easier and carried on, hopping into Baucom's car and ditching it in a parking lot a few miles away from her apartment. Just to be sure, he wiped the steering wheel, seats, door handles, the interior, and most of the exterior clean of fingerprints.

Later, Wallace sold the VCR to his associate Larry. He got $60, which he used to buy more cocaine.

Wallace caught a cab. Trekking back to his apartment, he was feeling smug about himself. He had got his drug fix while continuing to outsmart the police. The man who would become known as the Taco Bell Strangler had thought of everything. Or so he thought.

Wallace told police investigators: "...what happened was I had pulled the wrong lever (in the car) to open her (Baucom's) gas cap because I had to put gas into her car... the trunk came up, and I had to close it back down. And I pushed it down with my hand, and that's what I forgot.

The one thing he had forgotten: to wipe clean his finger and palm prints from Baucom's car trunk.

On the day that Wallace strangled Baucom, March 9, 1994, Baucom was scheduled to work, but did not show up. Baucom's unit director, Jeffrey Ellis, called Baucom's apartment several times but received no answer. He also called Baucom's mother, but she had not heard from Baucom either. Ellis checked with some of Baucom's co-workers, but no one had heard from her.

The next morning, Ellis became increasingly worried because Baucom was again scheduled to work but did not show up. He made some more calls to Baucom's mother and her aunt, but they still had not heard from Baucom. Ellis and Baucom's mother decided to contact the police department and report Betty Baucom as a missing person.

Ellis and another employee then headed to Baucom's apartment to do some private investigative work. They knocked on the door and looked in the windows. Everything looked normal and they left.

Meanwhile, the police responded to Ellis's and Mrs. Baucom's missing person report and checked out Baucom's apartment. Maintenance personnel let the police into Baucom's apartment. There, they discovered a grisly scene: Baucom's body lying face down on her bed with a towel around her neck. Approximately an hour after Ellis called the police, an officer approached him in the parking lot of the Bojangles' restaurant and told him the bad news. They had found Baucom's body.

Dr. Sullivan performed an autopsy on Baucom's body on March 11, 1994. He observed blunt-trauma injuries and evidence of strangulation, including a ligature in place around her neck. The ligature consisted of a small sheet or pillowcase in a knot with an additional towel wrapped between the skin of the neck and the sheet. Dr. Sullivan observed small abrasions and small contusions of the skin of the neck beneath the ligature and small hemorrhages in the conjunctiva.

Additionally, Dr. Sullivan observed abrasions on the left shoulder, both arms, the right upper chest, and the abdomen, and a blunt-trauma injury to the head, with an area of abrasion over the right forehead.

During the internal examination of Baucom's body, Dr. Sullivan observed a buildup of blood in the lungs, enlargement of the brain, small hemorrhages in the muscles in the front of the neck, and small hemorrhages in the lining of the voice box. He concluded that the cause of Baucom's death was strangulation and that the injuries observed were consistent with a struggle.

During their Baucom investigation, the police found a mess at Baucom's apartment. It had been noticeably plundered. They figured that by looking at the empty entertainment center and the cable wires leading to nowhere, the TV and VCR were missing. Her Pulsar was not in the parking lot.

Police squad cars cruised Charlotte's streets looking for Baucom's Pulsar, while police detectives searched the local pawn shops to see if someone had tried to sell the stolen items for cash.

Meanwhile, Wallace had returned to Henderson's apartment the same night when he knew Woods would be at work. Woods had left for work at 5 p.m. Henderson was on the phone talking with George Burrell, her cousin, when Wallace showed up at her door. Baby Tyrese was sleeping in the other room.

"Who's there?" Henderson called out.

"It's me, Henry...Henry Wallace."

Henderson told Burrell that she had to go to the door. Someone was there. She will be right back. Burrell didn't know who was at the door, but he did not worry because it seemed like she trusted the person.

Henderson approached the door.

"I thought you were supposed to be gone?" Henderson said.

"I'm getting ready to leave in a little bit," Wallace replied. "I have something to leave Lamar."

Henderson said okay and opened the door for Wallace. They stood at the door.

"Maybe you could call him and ask if it is okay to leave this merchandise with him," Wallace advised.

"Okay," Henderson said.

Henderson went back on the phone and told Burrell she would call him back because one of Squeaky's friends wanted her to call Squeaky Woods. She did not identify Wallace by name. Henderson hung up the phone and handed it to Wallace, who called Woods, but the line was busy.

"I'll call him back in a few minutes," Wallace told Henderson.

Henderson nodded and turned her back to Wallace.

"Do you have anything to drink?" Wallace asked Henderson.

"Yes," Henderson said.

Wallace watched Henderson with her back turned, reaching into the cabinet, getting a glass for his drink. He decided to make his move. He grabbed her in his familiar Boston chokehold and then calmly told her, "Listen, I won't hurt you, but this is a robbery. I'm gonna need all the money you have."

Henderson stared at Wallace in disbelief.

"I don't have but a little bit of money...about $15 in paper money and a bunch of coins," she said.

Where is it?" Wallace demanded.

"It's...it's in a Pringle can," Henderson responded.

Wallace thought for a second, then demanded, "Let's go into the bedroom."

"Can I hold my son?" Henderson pleaded.

"I don't know if that would be a good idea for what we're about to do," Wallace replied coldly. "Where's the money?"

Henderson gave Wallace the Pringle can filled with approximately twenty dollars in coins.

"There is no other money in the house," Henderson said.

Wallace took the money and glanced around the apartment. "I'll be taking the television and stereo as well," he said.

Then Wallace gave Henderson a chilling look and demanded, "Take off your clothes."

Henderson obliged and they had oral sex, then intercourse. Wallace told Henderson to stand up and put her clothes back on. After Henderson did that, she got on her knees and started praying.

"Why are you doing that? Wallace asked.

"I'm scared," Henderson mumbled.

Wallace lied. "I'm not going to hurt you. I got what I wanted, (sic) and I'm leaving."

Wallace asked Henderson for a hug and she hugged him. Wallace was sweating profusely. He went to the bathroom for a towel to wipe himself. He returned to Henderson who was now in her son's bedroom. Young Tyrese was sleeping on the bed. Henderson eyed Wallace and got nervous.

"There's…there's more stuff in the house you can take," Henderson blurted.

Wallace looked at Henderson, who grabbed her son, laid him across her chest, and turned his head away so he could not see what was going on.

Wallace squeezed the towel around Henderson's neck and choked her until her face turned red. Henderson passed out, but Wallace continued to have sex with her. Wallace grabbed another towel, wrapped it around Brandi's neck, squeezed, and proceeded to strangle her to death. Henderson's body crumpled to the floor. He then put her clothes and his back on.

Wallace picked up Henderson's body and put it on Tyrese's bed. Young Tyrese started crying. He got really loud, and Wallace thought he heard someone knock at the door. He got really scared and was afraid he would not be able to get out of the apartment with the merchandise he needed to buy dope.

Wallace gave Tyrese a pacifier and looked for something the baby could drink, but found nothing. Wallace then took another towel from the bathroom and tied the towel tight around Tyrese's neck so that it would be difficult for him to breathe and he would stop crying.

"I didn't want to tie it (the towel) too tight (just) enough to choke him…(just) enough to make it difficult for him to breath (sic)," Wallace would later claim.

Tyrese finally stopped crying. Lying next to his mother's body, the baby struggled to breathe.

Before leaving, Wallace took some food that had been delivered and the container of coins. He also took a television that was sitting on the floor. Wallace then ran into the living room, disconnected the stereo, and loaded it into Baucom's car. He later sold the television and stereo for $175.

Woods returned to the apartment around midnight. When he had left, Brandi Henderson and baby Tyrese were alone in the apartment, the front door was locked, and the apartment was neat and clean. When Woods returned, he found the front door unlocked, items scattered about the living room, and the stereo missing.

Concerned, Woods went through the apartment searching for his girlfriend. When he came to Tyrese's bedroom, he turned on the light. It was a shocking scene. Tyrese was sitting on the bed, gasping for air. A pair of shorts hung around his neck. Something white was coming out of his mouth.

Woods dashed to Tyrese and removed the shorts that were tied tightly around his neck. Woods saw that Henderson was lying face down on the bed, so he rolled her over on to her back. He saw that towels were tied around her neck and that her face was blue. Woods removed the two towels from Henderson's neck and then called 9-1-1. He moved Henderson's body from the bed to the floor and began administering CPR pursuant to instructions from the 9-1-1 operator. When police officers arrived, they checked Henderson's body. It was obvious Henderson was dead.

Tyrese was rushed to the Carolina Medical Center. Dr. Tom Brewer examined Tyrese in the emergency room, where the child was awake, breathing, and had stable vital signs. His injuries had caused him great pain and suffering, but, eventually, he became more alert and began interacting with his environment. However, his failure to pull away when stuck with a needle showed some evidence that he was not acting normally.

Dr. Brewer found red marks around Tyrese's neck consistent with something being tied around his neck. Further, Tyrese's altered mental status indicated his brain was not functioning normally because of some compromise of the blood flow to the brain. In addition, there was very fine bruising on his cheeks and eyelids caused by a buildup of blood pressure as a result of his jugular vein being blocked.

On March 10, 1994, Dr. James Sullivan performed an autopsy on Brandi Henderson's body. He observed evidence of strangulation including small hemorrhages in the eyes, over the skin of the face and neck, in the muscles in the neck, and in the lining of the voice box. Dr. Sullivan concluded that the cause of death was strangulation.

Between March 9 and March 11, 1994, there had been three murders in three days (Betty Baucom, Brandi Henderson, and Deborah Slaughter). Wallace had gotten reckless and extremely violent. He was on an orgy of killing and had abandoned the precautions that protected himself from arrest—wiping the murder scenes of evidence, spacing out the murders, and even bathing his victims. Henderson's murder had followed Baucom's murder by only hours, and two murders were similar. The pieces of the murder investigation were about to be fitted together and the connections the police had missed, exposed. Indeed, the case was about to break wide open.

Wallace, however, was not the least concerned. He continued to play his cold, calculating game. The day after Brandi Henderson's murder, Wallace was watching, with George Burrell, Henderson's cousin who had been on the phone with Henderson when Wallace showed up at her door, the 5 o'clock television news report about Henderson's murder.

Burrell was choked up about Brandi Henderson's death and Wallace tried to console him, telling him how sorry he was for his loss. Wallace touched Burrell and reassured him. Everything is going to be alright.

EIGHT

Take Down

But everything was not alright for the Charlotte Metropolitan Police Department (CPMD). Young Black women were dying and the public was outraged. They wanted answers. Feeling the pressure, Garry McFadden stepped up the investigation. Detectives interrogated possible suspects who operated in the area and could move easily unobserved in East Charlotte's Black community where the crimes were being committed. The police went back to the families and friends of the murder victims, hoping to establish some kind of connection between the victims. Maybe somebody worked with the killer or could have hung out with somebody who resembled the killer or knew someone who had a criminal record. Everything for Sergeant McFadden and the CMPD was on the table.

On March 10, 1994, two days after Brandi Henderson's murder, Sergeant McFadden called a meeting of his detectives to compare notes. McFadden was surprised to learn that Betty Baucom had been murdered in the same apartment complex as Brandi Henderson and that there were similar characteristics in the murders. Both victims were Black females; there was no forced entry in either case; and a ligature was used to murder in both cases.

Characteristics in the Vanessa Mack, Baucom, and Henderson murders also matched. Could the murderer possibly be someone who knew all three victims? The police asked the family and friends of the victims for the names of people who might have been allowed into the houses of the victims. One name showed up on all the lists: Henry Louis Wallace.

The police brought in Brandi Henderson's boyfriend, Verness Lamar "Squeaky" Woods, for questioning about his girlfriend's murder. They had cleared him of being a possible suspect, but they wanted to know if there was anybody besides Woods she would let into the apartment. He gave the police three names, one of which was Henry Wallace.

Police learned that Betty Baucom had worked with Wallace's girlfriend at Bojangles on Central Avenue. Audrey Spain and Shawna Hawk worked for Wallace at Taco Bell. Michelle Stinson met him there, while Brandi Henderson had worked with him at the Golden Corral. To Sheriff McFadden it looked like too much of a coincidence. The police were possibly on to something.

On March 11, 1994, the police found Betty Baucom's vehicle. They lifted a palm print from the trunk of the car and compared it with Wallace's prints. They matched. A search of the police criminal records revealed that there was an outstanding warrant for his arrest on a larceny offense. The CMPD went looking for Wallace.

Wallace, however, was not through with his violent rampage. His crack habit was out of control, and after killing Brandi Henderson, he went looking for his next victim and fix. Wallace decided to pay a visit to Deborah Slaughter. Slaughter had an 18-year-old son living in Atlanta and, at 35, was the oldest of four children. She worked as a deli clerk at a Harris Teeter supermarket. Slaughter had once worked at the Bojangles on Central Avenue with Wallace's girlfriend, Sadie McKnight. That is where she had met Wallace.

Slaughter had moved from Florida to Atlanta where she owned her own business selling perfume, makeup, and other women's accessories. She then moved to Charlotte where she was joined by other family members. Linda Moore, her sister, says neither she nor any of her other family ever recall hearing Wallace's name. "Debra (sic) never mentioned him to any of us, and none of us ever met him," Moore said.

Moore was very close to her sister, although they did not see each other much. "Debra (sic) was beautiful," Moore recalled. "She was a happy person and a nice person as well." Family members remember Slaughter as a tall, strong woman, with an infectious laugh, a great sense of humor and a beautiful singing voice that shone in the church choir.

One woman who knew Slaughter said, "She could beat the tambourine like it was nobody's business." She referred to Slaughter as the "Black Lucy" as in famed comedian Lucille Ball. "I will never forget Debra (sic) Slaughter," said the woman. "She was one of a kind."

Slaughter had been living in Charlotte at the Glen Hollow Apartments for about six months when Wallace showed up on March 12, 1994. Like most of Wallace's other murdered victims, Slaughter knew and trusted him and would readily let him into her apartment.

Once inside, Wallace asked Slaughter to get him something to drink. As Slaughter turned around, Wallace put a towel he had brought with him which was tucked under his jacket around Slaughter's neck and tightened it. They tussled and Slaughter fell to her knees. Wallace ordered her to remove her clothes and perform oral sex on him. Later, Wallace remembered Slaughter saying, "I don't do that; you might as well go ahead and kill me."

Wallace tightened the towel and asked Slaughter if she wanted to change her mind. Wallace then forced Slaughter to remove her clothes and he raped her. After they were finished, Wallace told Slaughter to put her clothes back on. Slaughter confronted Wallace, raging, "My suspicions of you are confirmed. You are the one who has been strangling all those women." Wallace was taken aback by Slaughter's aggression, but he denied it.

Slaughter became even more insistent. Wallace told Slaughter to shut up, open her wallet, and give him what money she had. Slaughter handed him forty dollars from the wallet. Wallace knew Slaughter carried a knife in her purse at all times, so he asked her to empty the contents of her purse onto the floor, which she did.

The knife fell out and he kicked it away. Suddenly, Slaughter hit Wallace and screamed for the police. Wallace put a sock in her mouth, then tightened the towel around Slaughter's neck until she fell to the floor. Slaughter started kicking and Wallace tightened the towel some more. He tried sitting on top of Slaughter's legs to keep her from kicking and alerting the neighbor living downstairs.

Wallace went to the bathroom to retrieve another towel, which he tied with the first one around Slaughter's neck. He stabbed Slaughter with the knife from her purse in the abdomen and chest. "I caught her arm and I grabbed the knife from (sic) other, and I stabbed her about twenty times," Wallace later explained. "It was a little knife shaped kind of like a dagger."

The violence of the crime was actually much more brutal. The number of times that Wallace stabbed Slaughter was later counted by the authorities at thirty-eight. Wallace then washed the knife clean, wiped his fingerprints from it, and placed it back with the contents of Slaughter's purse on the floor.

Wallace left Slaughter's apartment to purchase crack cocaine. He returned a few hours later with a glass pipe and some crack rocks. He marched past Slaughter, who lay on the floor, dead, and went into the bathroom, where he calmly smoked the crack. When finished, he grabbed a Chicago White Sox jacket, a baseball cap, and a butcher knife and left the apartment. He threw the items away after leaving the apartment.

Kevin Sherill, an associate of Wallace's stopped by a Fast Fare, and as he was leaving the store, he saw a panicky looking Wallace in the parking lot.

Wallace said to Sherill, "Have you heard the news?"

"What news?" Sherill replied.

"Someone told me Brandi Henderson was murdered."

They rushed over to Sherrill's place to watch the 5 p.m. news, and what Wallace told Sherill was confirmed. The newscaster read Brandi's name, and a photo of her and of little Tyrese, her baby, who Wallace had choked but survived, was shown on the screen.

On March 12, 1994, Slaughter's mother, Lovey Slaughter, headed to her daughter's apartment to return a picture she had borrowed a few days before. Lovey had a key to the apartment and anticipated letting herself in because Slaughter was supposed to be at work. When Lovey arrived, she knocked on the door and got no response. She put the key into the lock and discovered that the door was unlocked.

As Lovey walked into the apartment, she saw Slaughter's body lying on the floor. She was not alarmed, though. Slaughter had been suffering from back pain and she had an appointment with a chiropractor that day. Deborah had stretched out to ease the pain in her back, Lovey assumed. Then she saw the pool of blood and frantically called 9-1-1.

Officer Ronnie Chambers of the Charlotte-Mecklenburg Police Department entered Slaughter's apartment and found a purse with its contents scattered on the floor. The police officer then noticed Slaughter's body lying on the floor face up. She had been viciously raped, beaten, stabbed, and choked to death, with the two towels tied around her neck and a white fabric shoved down Slaughter's windpipe. Chambers also observed several puncture wounds in Slaughter's chest. The police would soon determine that the Slaughter murder exhibited characteristics similar to the Mack, Henderson, and Baucom cases.

Meanwhile, Henry Wallace was in a bad state. He had not slept for three days. He was on edge and jittery. A couple of times he had taken a crack hit and had gone into convulsions. Wallace later recalled at his police interrogation, "My body was shaking. I fell against the wall, and I remember walking up and I was like, damn, that was a good hit. That felt really good. And then the next time, it really hit me hard. I was in the bedroom and I fell, and I just fell flat, and I passed out. I knew I had to be out for a few minutes. I had a homemade gun, and at that point is when I tried to commit suicide."

When Wallace came to, he ran to the bathroom to get a gun and shoot himself, but he craved another hit and could not do it. Wallace never got to the point again where he thought about killing himself.

But his drug problem and lack of sleep were making him increasingly paranoid. When he went back to Baucom's Pulsar car, he thought he saw an undercover woman police officer, whom he recognized, following him. She was driving a Mercury Cougar and Wallace believed she worked for the vice squad. He could not remember her name.

Wallace had bought some crack, had taken a hit, and was looking for a more secure place to smoke some more. He thought he found the place in a little utility booth behind the Black Eye Pea Restaurant. He had forgotten his lighter, however, and when he turned around to go to the car and get it, he saw the woman he thought was the undercover police officer. He ran to the utility booth and locked himself in. He heard a helicopter circling around and thought he had been spotted.

Then he heard a knock on the utility shed door. It was a white man who said he was homeless, but Wallace did not believe him. The white man said he was going to Monroe, North Carolina, and had left his shirt in the booth. Wallace opened the door and let the man get the shirt. But Wallace was wary. He still suspected he was a cop.

Wallace thought he heard the white man talking to a woman and questioned the man about it. The man denied it. Wallace also thought he heard footsteps outside the booth. He continued to take crack cocaine, but every time he took a hit, he would pass out. Upon awakening, he saw shadows in the corner moving toward him, making him even more paranoid.

On March 14,1994, two days after Slaughter's murder, Dr. Sullivan performed an autopsy on her body. During the external examination, he observed a ligature around Slaughter's neck and a sock balled up and stuffed into her mouth, holding her mouth open. There was evidence of strangulation, including the ligature around Slaughter's neck and hemorrhages in the conjunctiva. The ligature was comprised of two towels, the inner towel encircled around the neck and the outer towel tied tightly in a single knot.

Dr. Sullivan also observed blunt-trauma injuries, including abrasions of the skin of the face and a single scalp contusion. Additionally, the medical examiner observed sharp-trauma injuries caused by thirty-eight stab wounds to the chest and abdomen. Three of the stab wounds caused injury to the heart and twelve of the stab wounds caused injury to the left lung. Each of these stab wounds could have been fatal.

Stab wounds had also caused injury to the liver and stomach. Dr. Sullivan concluded that Slaughter's death was caused by multiple stab wounds with strangulation as a contributing factor in the death.

The CMPD had the evidence it needed to arrest and charge Wallace with murder. Through the evening of March 11 and the following day, police officers staked out the Glen Hollow Apartments on North Sharon Amity Road where they believed Wallace was living. On March 12, during their search for Wallace, investigators learned that Deborah Slaughter's body had been discovered in her apartment. The police hunt for Wallace now took on a sense of urgency.

The police tracked Wallace down to a friend's house on Winterfield Place in East Charlotte. He was arrested hiding in a bathroom and cuffed between 5:30 and 6:00 p.m. for an outstanding warrant for larceny. He had failed to appear in court on a charge he shoplifted a $49 sweater from Belk's in Eastland Mall.

Wallace was brought into the law enforcement center, or LEC, where a small brigade of plainclothes police officers waited for his arrival with some excitement. At the LEC, Wallace was led into an interrogation room and was seated at a chair before a long bare table under fluorescent lighting. The police officers introduced themselves and told him he was there because of the larceny charge.

Wallace was advised of his Miranda rights and then the police sprung on Wallace as to why he was really brought in to the LEC. They told of the evidence they had connecting him to the murders of the nine back women: Love, Hawk, Spain, Jumper, Stinson, Mack, Baucom, Henderson, and Slaughter, whom he murdered less than forty-eight hours before his arrest. They showed photos of him attempting to use Mack's ATM card at teller machines and the matching palm print from Baucom's car. At this point, Wallace was not talking, but eventually he did talk.

And talk, he did, confessing to the murders of the women. The police spent a Saturday night, about ten hours, interrogating Wallace, putting all of his confessions on tape. According to the arresting police officer, Wallace appeared calm and collected, seemed "a little wrinkled," and did not put up a fight. The interrogation would also reveal Wallace's murder of two other unfortunate women: Tashanda Bethea and Sharon Nance.

McFadden walked in and out of the interrogation room, observing Wallace and listening to him respond to the interrogators' questions. "He was very cunning and charismatic, very attentive to his surroundings and the people with whom he was interacting," McFadden recalled.

"I could see how he could manipulate his way into the lives of his victims."

When one of the investigating police officers asked Wallace, "Why did you decide to tell us this?" Wallace responded, "It's got to end. Everything has got to end."

When the police officer followed up with, "So you are doing this because you want to? Wallace answered bluntly, "I'm doing this because, first of all, I knew that it would be a very long time before I hit the streets again from the evidence you guys have. I knew you had enough to convict me of two of the murders, and if I'm convicted of two, I might be convicted of all of them. I might as well tell the truth. I'm never going to hit the streets again anyway. I'll never live a day outside the penitentiary again."

The detectives focused on the most damning evidence against Wallace: the palm and fingerprints on Baucom's car. Wallace was confident he had wiped Baucom's car clean of prints. But when one of the detectives said, "We got your prints," Wallace became agitated and blurted out, "No, you don't have my prints from inside the car." One of the detectives responded, "We have them outside the car." Caught off guard, Wallace shut down.

One investigator asked him if he might be schizophrenic since he had to admit that he did not seem like a bad person. Wallace's answer was curt, "No. There's only one Henry…a (bad) Henry."

At that point, Detective Tony Rice entered the room and changed interrogation tactics. Rice and Wallace looked at each other, and Wallace said, "Tony, I fucked up."

How did Bad Henry know Tony Rice's name? "It shows you how cunning Wallace is," McFadden explained." He is very attentive and listens well. Someone in the room mentioned Tony's name, and Wallace picked up."

Rice asked Wallace, "Are you a Christian?"

"I like to think I am," Wallace responded.

"Okay, let's say a prayer," Rice said.

Wallace and Rice prayed together.

After they had prayed together, Wallace's resistance to the questioning seemed to crumble. He asked Rice for a piece of paper. He was given the sheet of paper and started to write down names. The interrogating detectives looked at the piece of paper and at each other and did not know what to say. Wallace had not been connected to any of women listed on the paper.

They had the missing link to the cases. Up to that point, Wallace had not been directly connected to any of the murders. Moreover, they did not have Valencia Jumper in the file. The detectives asked Wallace who she was? He said that she was the one who died in the fire he had set. Up to that point, Jumper's death had been considered accidental.

For about ten hours, Wallace spoke into a recording microphone, explaining the disturbing details of his horrendous crimes. He talked about how he knew the women, how they trusted him, how he got into their houses, how they turned their backs on him, the gruesome details of their killings, including how he applied what he called the "Boston choke" to render his victims unconscious, their final terrifying words, and how he exited the crime scenes.

Although he talked about his desperate search for money as his drug habit worsened, Wallace insisted his motive for murder was not sex. He had fantasies of controlling his victims through the power of sex, but the money was more important. As he was fired from one job and another, the only way he knew how to get money was from his unsuspecting friends.

Wallace talked about the murder of Brandi Henderson. "I went to the bathroom and grabbed a towel. I folded the towel and put it around her neck. And that's when I strangled her to death."

Among his victims was Caroline Love, missing person, whose body had never been found. Wallace had met Love through his girlfriend, Sadie McKnight. Wallace and Sadie had filed a missing report for Love.

Wallace described Love's murder in a matter-of-fact tone, "She was laying on the sofa, and I came up behind her, kissed her on the cheek. I can't remember if I used my hands or if I used another object to strangle her to death."

Wallace spoke about the great lengths he went to cover up the murders, but he had become increasingly careless as his drug habit worsened. The police had used rape kits to collect evidence in the murders. The results had been missed in the massive backlog of evidence. When test results were finally completed, five of the victims showed traces of DNA consistent with that of Henry Wallace.

Later, on March 13, 1994, after the police were through interrogating Wallace and getting his confession, Wallace directed investigators to the site where he had dumped Love's body. Subsequently, Dr. James Sullivan, forensic pathologist and medical examiner employed by the Medical Examiner's Office of Mecklenburg County, went to the area of Statesville Road to recover Love's skeletal remains. Dr. Sullivan determined that the cause of death was homicide by means of strangulation.

Also on March 13, police officers interviewed Wallace about the death of Betty Baucom. They talked about the property he had taken from Baucom's house and how it had ended up in the possession of a man named only as Larry.

Investigators talked to Wallace about knowing Betty Baucom and the two other women he had killed two days before, Vanessa Mack and Brandi Henderson. Wallace was asked if he knew where Baucom lived and he said no. Could he explain how his fingerprints were found on Baucom's car. Wallace got defensive, answering: "You didn't get my prints in her car. I know you didn't."

The interrogator asked: How did it look with him having items belonging to Betty Baucom and fingerprints on her car? Wallace began crying and mumbled about the hard life he had led.

"What are you talking about?" the interrogator asked.

Wallace's answer was full of self-pity. "It's hard trying to get ahead in the world when you make six or seven dollars and other people get more money for doing the same job as you."

The interrogator asked what this had to do with the death of Baucom, Mack, and Henderson, and Wallace started to cry again. "Why are you crying?" The police officer asked. Wallace answered: 'I'm crying because you think I killed these women. I wouldn't hurt anyone."

"Well, did you kill these women?" the interrogator asked.

Wallace did not respond. He just kept crying.

The interrogator tried a new line of questioning, asking him what he knew about the dead women? Wallace stated that he knew some of the women, but not all.

The interrogator had been looking at Wallace's hands and saw what looked like new scratch marks on the top of his right hand. He also saw that the knuckles of his left hand looked bruised. The interrogator touched Wallace's right hand and asked him what happened here. Wallace did not answer and continued to cry.

They next talked about whether Wallace had a girlfriend. "Yes," Wallace said. But she had put him out of their apartment.

"Did you hurt her?" the interrogator asked.

"One time," Wallace revealed.

He had choked her because she had bit him on his stomach. Wallace pulled up his shirt and showed the interrogator a scar on the right side of his stomach area. Wallace explained that he had choked her only after she would not stop biting him.

"Had you had any other physical contact with her?" the interrogator asked.

No, was the response.

The interrogator again asked Wallace how he got the items that came from Betty Baucom's house and Wallace gave the same response as before: from two street people, then he traded them for cocaine from Larry.

The interrogation switched to asking about Wallace's drug use and Wallace said he was doing cocaine, sometimes fifty to sixty dollars'-worth a day.

That was not a lot, the interrogator noted, and then he asked if Wallace would do anything bad while doing cocaine. "No, I would not, and I was never out of my head," Wallace replied, boasting: "I would always be in control."

"So, what would cause you to do bad things?" the interrogator asked.

No response from Wallace.

The interrogation came back to the deaths of Baucom, Mack, and Henderson. Wallace got smart-alecky. "I know a lot of dead people, don't you (sic)?" he asked.

"Isn't it kind of strange that all the women I ask you about are dead and all died in the same manner?" the interrogator asked.

Wallace quipped again: "I know a lot of dead people."

Wallace was getting brave. "All you got is on the Betty Baucom case."

"Is it?" the interrogator shot back.

"Well, that's all you said you had," Wallace responded.

The interrogation moved again to the prints on Betty Baucom's car and the fact that he had in his possession items taken from her house.

"How do you think this looks?" the interrogator asked.

"There's a lot of people in jail for things they didn't do," Wallace replied. "The system is bad."

"Don't you want to tell us what you know, what involvement you had?" the interrogator asked.

Wallace again began to cry. "I didn't do anything to them," he insisted.

With the interrogation going nowhere, the interrogator got up and left the room. The interrogation was over. It had taken fifty-two minutes.

Wallace eventually confessed to two other murders beside the nine in Charlotte: Tashanda Bethea in Barnwell and Sharon Nance in Charlotte. Wallace had one other caveat for the police. He took the police to where he had dumped Caroline Love's body in the wooded area of the 9500 block of Statesville Road.

Wallace had had a brutal two-year run of murders, and this was it in terms of the murders to which Wallace confessed. Wallace, however, would be suspected of other murders, especially unsolved murders in the areas where he was stationed while in the navy. Nothing has ever been proved, even though many of those victims fall into the same age and economic range as the ten victims Wallace is known to have murdered. And Wallace was not talking.

NINE

The Arrest

On March 13, 1994, over a ten-hour period, Wallace described in chilling detail via a tape-recorded conversation, how, when, and where he had murdered ten Charlotte women and one other from Barnwell, South Carolina. Wallace did steal items from his victims, primarily to get money to support his drug habit, but he told police detectives that power, domination, and sexual gratification were primary motivations for his killing spree. After the confession and a brief conversation with his girlfriend, Wallace was put in jail on suicide watch.

Was Sadie McKnight, his girlfriend, complicit in his serial killing? In their case study of Wallace, *Lives Interrupted*, criminologists Charisse Coston and J.B. Kuhns write, "According to police investigators, his girlfriend did not know that he was a serial killer, which again is not entirely unusual. Serial killers often have girlfriends during their killing spree, and some even have wives. Albert de Salvo, also known as the Boston Strangler, for instance, was married with two children."

On March 15, 1994, Wallace made his first court appearance before a packed room of reporters and curious and interested spectators. Virginia Love, Caroline Love's sister, was there. They had found her sister's corpse two days before. After an emotional outburst, Virginia had to be escorted from the courtroom. She told reporters: "I thought about my mother. She had a heart attack. She died worrying about her (daughter, Caroline Love). Before she had a chance to find out what happened, it killed her."

News 36, the Charlotte television news channel, managed to get an interview with Wallace. When asked if he had anything to say to the victims, Wallace responded that he wanted them to know he would like to make a statement, but he needed to clear that with his attorney first.

Dee Sumpter found out about Wallace's arrest from the television news. "I saw Wallace's photo on the screen, then my daughter," Sumpter recalled. "It was like being punched in the stomach. I fell on the floor with such force that I hit my head and started bleeding."

Wallace's mother, Lottie Mae Wallace, and his sister, Yvonne, were shocked as well by the news that their son and brother was a suspected serial killer. They also learned of Wallace's arrest through news reports. In an interview at her home in Barnwell, South Carolina, Lottie lamented, "It's like you're in a dream, and you're eventually going to wake up—that's how it seems to me." Yvonne expressed sympathy with the victims, stating, "We feel sorry for them that these things happened. Those lives didn't have to be taken."

Neighbors who knew the affable, friendly Henry Wallace could not believe that he had been arrested for serial killing. "I think it's just really hard for a lot of people to comprehend how ten women just perished like that. And no one really knew," said Robert Kelly, who owned a dress shop.

A neighbor of Wallace when he lived in Barnwell, South Carolina, who spoke anonymously, found it hard to believe someone from Barnwell would do the things of which Wallace was accused. "He was a guy I felt had it all together," the neighbor lamented. But people who knew

Wallace in Charlotte said they noticed a change in him after he started taking drugs, but no one thought he was a killer.

On March 13, the day after his confession, police investigators put Wanda Harrison, the mother of Wallace's baby, on the phone with Henry Wallace. Wallace told Harrison that he wanted to see his baby. Harrison had not seen Wallace since September 1993. Harrison could not believe what she saw on the television news. The man arrested for murdering ten women was nothing like the man she remembered, nice to her, always wanting to help, buying presents for the baby. After the baby was born, Wallace came to the hospital, bringing a friendship ring for her. Harrison lamented what she would tell her daughter about her father when the daughter was older.

The Charlotte community breathed a sigh of relief with the capture of killer Henry Louis Wallace. The police reassured the women of East Charlotte that they were now safe with Henry Louis Wallace behind bars. But it was not until March 9, 1994, that the police had warned the residents of East Charlotte that they had a serial killer in their midst. Charlotte police chief Dennis Nowicki acknowledged that the Charlotte Metropolitan Police Department (CMPD) had not spotted a link among the murders sooner and he apologized. But Nowicki also added that, in the CMPD's defense, there were enough differences in the cases to steer them off Wallace's trail.

For many in the community, however, an apology was not enough, and Nowicki's explanation was a lame excuse. The critics accused the police of racism and neglecting the crimes because they involved young Black women from lower economic backgrounds. As Dee Sumpter bluntly put it, "The victims were not prominent people with social-economic status. They weren't special. And they were black (sic)."

Criticism of the police came from a variety of quarters. Darrell Alleyne, a retired police officer from New York who was living in Charlotte called for Sergeant McFadden's dismissal, arguing that Wallace should have at least been a suspect in the Caroline Love disappearance in 1992, never mind what happened in any of the other killings. Meanwhile, Charlotte's chapter of the National Organization of Women called for an independent counsel to investigate the police department.

In May of 1994, Dee Sumpter of Mothers of Murdered Offspring (MOM-O), asked Charlotte's City Council to investigate the police department. Sumpter said her organization would be willing to work with the CMPD to help train police investigators to be more sensitive to the kinds of issues they were overlooking, increase communication between investigators, and help increase information exchanges between the homicide department and patrol divisions.

Police were surprised at the backlash following Wallace's arrest. "I was not prepared for this reaction," admitted Jack Boger, acting Charlotte-Mecklenburg Police Chief. "We were focused on wrapping up the case. Now I know what to expect."

Boger and several other police investigators held a news conference on March 17, 1994, where they brought along a large chart showing each of the nine Charlotte murders Wallace was accused of committing. Dan Steger, Assistant Manager for the city of Charlotte, told the press, "The excellent work of our department (the CMPD) brought this case to closure within forty-eight hours of the identification of the primary suspect." What Steger left out was that by this time the prime suspect had allegedly murdered the nine women in Charlotte.

Sumpter told the press that the police should have focused on individuals who worked with her daughter at the Taco Bell restaurant on Central Avenue. Wallace had hired her daughter, Shawna Hawk. Boger claimed the CMPD was never told about a potential connection between the restaurant and the Hawk murder. Boger revealed that Wallace did not become a suspect until police discovered the body of Brandi Henderson on March 9. That was the first time the police had evidence linking a murder to an earlier one.

In the late 1990s, WBTV, a Charlotte television station, produced an investigative documentary on the Wallace case titled *Bodies of Evidence: The Wallace Investigation.* According to the expert criminal profilers and homicide detectives on the show, police should have recognized early on that they were dealing with a methodical serial killer because of the common elements of the case.

The comments by the experts on the show were scathing. Cyril Wecht, noted forensic pathologist, charged, "I believe there was professional malpractice in the (Wallace) case. (The police) didn't do the job, didn't see a pattern of strangulation."

Vernon Geberth, at the time a homicide consultant and a retired 23-year veteran of the NYPD, told the WBTV presenter, "Investigators missed an obvious serial pattern. This pattern should have been recognized in 1993." Geberth added, "After just two strangulations I certainly would have linked (the case) to one person (because of) the strangulation aspect. No question about it." Geberth believes the police missed linking the strangulations; that is, linking the Shawna Hawk, Aubrey Spain, Vanessa Mack, and Michelle Stinson murders to one killer.

At the March 17 meeting, Rick Sanders of the CMPD said strangulation deaths are not common and that the Wallace murders did not arouse suspicions. Sanders does have a point. The percentage of strangulations for all murders in North Carolina over a three-year period was as follows: 1989 (4 percent), 1990 (2.5 percent) and 1991 (2.9 percent). Geberth, however, argued, "Three black (sic) females murdered in their homes, with no forced entry. That's bad. That would point to a stalker. You know you are dealing with one offender because of the condensed spread of the homicide."

The medical examiner made mistakes, according to the documentary, the most egregious being the ruling that Valcencia Jumper's death was due to carbon monoxide poisoning after a fire at her home. Later at his police interrogation, Wallace would confess to setting the fire and to killing Jumper.

To show that the CMPD was being proactive in apprehending criminals, the FBI announced a new task force that involved a partnership with the CMPD, as well as the FBI, the local Sheriff's Department, the North Carolina Department of Corrections, and the North Carolina State Bureau of Investigation. The focus of the new task force would be violent predators and alleged killers like Henry Wallace.

The FBI revealed that the task force had been in operation three weeks, and that, in that time, fourteen people had been arrested and were facing the prospect of tougher prison sentences. The revolving prison doors are being closed for those who are caught and convicted by this task force, the FBI maintained.

Louis Freeh, FBI director, who made a special trip to Charlotte to announce the creation of the task force, told the press, "Once those people are interdicted, apprehended and detained, you will see a marked decrease in criminal activity in the area."

Meanwhile, the court was deciding what kind of DNA testing would be used in the Wallace trial. The FBI revealed that its lab was looking to see if there was a DNA fingerprint for Wallace in his murder case. Wallace's defense had asked the court for blood samples in case they wanted to hire experts to do their own testing. A judge would have to rule on the size of the sample, and there could be a big fight over the accuracy of the DNA. For example, could the DNA match only one person in five billion, or could there be 100 men in Charlotte who might match the DNA at the crime scenes?

Wallace's defense attorneys did not trust the accuracy of the DNA testing method the court planned to use. Judge Robert Johnston was told the DNA tests would take four months to complete. This meant that Wallace's trial would not begin until well into 1995.

Police investigators continued to look for evidence that could strengthen their case against Wallace. In September 1994, they searched a field in East Charlotte using a metal detector. They were looking for a piece of jewelry Wallace may have tossed in the area behind the Granville Apartments where he once lived.

On May 9, 1994, Charlotte Council member Hoyle Martin warned that he would ask for an outside probe if he was not satisfied with the CMPD's internal review of the Wallace case. Hoyle told the press he would drop his call for an outside audit if he found the CMPD probe into the Wallace case to be impartial. He added, however, that he did not think the internal review would be impartial.

A least one Charlotte City Council woman, Lynne Wheeler, thought the CMPD handled the Wallace case fairly and professionally, but expressed concern that a racially charged case like that of Wallace's could have a negative impact on local race relations. "It may be necessary to conduct an outside professional audit to clear the air," Wheeler told the *Charlotte Observer*. "If we resist an audit, it may appear we have something to hide when I'm sure we don't."

The call for an independent audit, however, faded after Police Chief Nowicki warned that an outside audit would hinder their case against Wallace. Charlotte Council members voted 10 to 1 to wait until Nowicki completed the internal review of the Wallace investigation. They would then receive the review in a closed session.

Police Chief Nowicki continued to walk a tightrope in the aftermath of the investigation, contending that, "I'm also certain there were no deliberate failures on the part of any of our officers. You have to understand that police agencies experience serial killers very infrequently."

Dee Sumpter, perhaps the most vocal critic of the police handling of the Wallace investigation, demanded a speedy trial and that the police admit there were "major discrepancies" in the Wallace investigation.

Sumpter met with noted civil rights activist Jesse Jackson in June 1994. Jackson said he would call for a U.S. Justice Department investigation. "We're facing a lot of controversy here in the city (Charlotte) in regard to the violence and injustice that's here," Jackson told the press. "Those mothers who lost their children have a right to get the best answers."

The North Carolina Chapter of the NAACP got involved with the Wallace case. Kelly Alexander, Jr. came before the Charlotte City Council and demanded, "I stand before you this evening to ask what has this council done to review the conduct of the police investigation and to take corrective action where necessary." Alexander added: "A lot of people believe that the police dropped the ball. And if they did drop it, we have a problem within our police investigative system that needs to be addressed." Nasif Majeed was the only council member to respond to Alexander's presentation.

Meanwhile, Wallace was held without bond in the Mecklenburg County jail. On April 4, 1994, Wallace appeared in Mecklenburg Superior Court. He was indicted for killing nine women in Charlotte. Wallace pleaded not guilty to the charges of murder, rape, sexual assault, armed robbery, larceny, and arson.

On August 11, Wallace appeared again in Mecklenburg Superior Court shackled at the ankles and wearing a blue sports jacket and shirt, maroon tie, khaki pants, and blue sneakers. He answered "not guilty" thirty-six times as the Assistant District Attorney asked for his plea on each count of the previous April indictment. Wallace's defense attorneys, Isabel Day and Jim Cooney, asked Superior Court Judge Marlene Hiatt for more time to file a notice of an insanity defense and a motion to suppress statements Wallace made to police after his arrest. They also asked the court to prohibit the state from destroying physical evidence that could be used in DNA testing and left open the possibility that they could use an insanity defense in defending Wallace.

Wallace was competently defended by lawyers Isabel Day and Jim Cooney. Day was Charlotte's public defender, a position she would hold for three decades. Day admitted the case consumed her life. "To try to explain how a serial killer is made was, I think, one of the most difficult things that I've ever done," Day told *Charlotte Magazine* on July 19, 2010. "It was a life-changing case for me. There were so many victims—including Henry himself, in my opinion—and so much tragedy, so much horror, really, and sadness. So many lives affected. It was overwhelming to try to grasp." When asked about her defense of Wallace, Day said: "All I could do is care about him as a human being. I do not see him as a monster that other people saw."

Cooney, an Irish Catholic from Chicago and a member of the prestigious Charlotte law firm of Kennedy Covington and Lobdell was described as one of North Carolina's leading defense lawyers in capital cases. According to the *Charlotte Observer*, he had handled thirteen capital cases, putting him on the "A" list of lawyers willing to defend murder suspects. Cooney's record of never having lost a client to execution would be tested in the Wallace trial.

Cooney was on record as opposing the death penalty, though he did recognize that the state's constitution allows it. "I've always felt that if we're going to have a death penalty, then I have an obligation to see that it's done correctly," Cooney told the *North Carolina Super Lawyers Magazine* in 2010.

In an interview with the *Charlotte Observer*, Cooney explained his approach to defense work. "You got to see them (defendants) as people. You got to love your client. If you don't love them, there is no way you can save their life ...They become a member of your family. I got Christmas cards from death row. We send them Christmas cards."

Day's and Cooney's client, Henry Wallace, awaited his trial at the Mecklenburg County Jail, where he led a routine and solitary life. He occupied a windowless cell the size of a walk-in closet. Twice a day, two officers shackled him and allowed him half an hour of exercise up and down the jail corridors. At 5:30 in the morning, a breakfast of milk, juice, eggs or grits, and a meat was delivered to his cell. Lunch at 11 a.m. included Kool-Aid, a green vegetable, a meat, and a fruit. Much the same dinner arrived at 4:30 p.m.

Wallace was transferred to a new cell in October 1995 after a fire broke out at the Mecklenburg County jail. The fire set off an alarm, and it was put out quickly. No one was injured, but the fire caused damage to the walls of the cell and to the bed linen. The authorities blamed Wallace for the fire, saying that he used a lighter to set fire to a wad of papers. Lighters are not allowed in the jail and authorities said they would launch an investigation to find out how Wallace got one.

It was not the first time Wallace had gotten into trouble. Earlier in March 1995, he had locked a deputy in his cell. Wallace was in a room adjoining his cell when a deputy came in to check on him. Wallace came up from behind the deputy, shut and then locked the door. Wallace's punishment—he was confined for more than a month to his cell for all but one hour a day.

Then in April 1995, Wallace got into a fight with James Morris Love, the brother of Caroline Love, one of Wallace's victims. Love had been sentenced to ten years in federal prison for drug conspiracy, racketeering, and firearms convictions and was awaiting transfer to a federal facility. When the fight broke out, Wallace was shackled and handcuffed. A nurse who examined Wallace said he had received abrasions and a bump on his wrists, but that would not keep him from going to court.

Wallace's case had made him a national celebrity and he received queries from a host of prominent journalists, including Tom Brokaw and Forrest Sawyer. Wallace had been advised not to speak without his attorney present. Wallace's popularity with the public prompted Dee Sumpter to file a wrongful death suit on April 20, 1994, preventing Wallace from making money from his life story.

Sumpter sought damages from Wallace for the murder of her daughter, Shawna Hawk. Specifically, Sumpter's lawsuit sought $6,000 for funeral expenses and hospital costs. The suit also demanded that Wallace be forced to compensate Sumpter for depriving her of daughter Shawna's company. Sumpter's attorney, Monroe Whitesides, told the *Charlotte Observer*, "It's a really tragic situation that this guy can gain notoriety for no other reason than that he killed a lot (sic) people."

On May 9, Sumpter appeared on *The Donahue Show* to advocate for a Son of Sam law in North Carolina. Such laws, named after convicted serial killer David Berkowitz, make it illegal for criminals to profit from crimes, books, and movies they may have done after the crime. North Carolina representative Davis Balmer, a Republican from Mecklenburg County, indicated he planned to introduce a bill to make the Son of Sam law legal in North Carolina.

With Wallace's name now well-known across the country, police departments began to search their cold case files to see if any of them had a connection to Wallace. Allendale police chief James Grant came to Charlotte on March 21, 1994, to question Henry Wallace in connection with the May 1987 strangulation of Pernetta Mew Riddle, who was raped in her apartment even though it was locked. Evidence from the crime scene led to Wallace. Grant said he planned to file charges against Wallace, although he did not specify what those charges would be. Grant never did file charges against Wallace.

The thought of Wallace possibly getting away with murder spawned more soul searching on the part of law enforcement. Officials lamented the fact that Wallace had committed crimes in North and South Carolina since the late 1980s, which, if the police had investigated, would have got him arrested as a career criminal and resulted in more severe punishment that would have kept him in jail. Hugh Munn, a spokesman for the South Carolina State Law Enforcement Division, told the *State* newspaper that Wallace's entire criminal record was in a central criminal history computer file that was available to law enforcement. That included Wallace's burglary conviction in Washington State, the attempted rape charge in Allendale in 1990, and a 1992 rape charge in Rock Hill, South Carolina.

Charlotte police did not find out about Wallace's background until they had picked him up for shoplifting in early February 1994. He was released with a written promise to appear in court a month later. When he did not appear, another warrant was issued. Wallace's luck ran out when he was arrested on the shoplifting charge after the police connected the dots in the murder case.

Wallace had confessed to the murders, but in November 1994, Wallace's attorneys filed a motion to suppress the interviews he had done with police investigators on March 12, 1994. His defense argued that he had been coerced into making the confession and that he had not been administered his Miranda rights until 10 p.m.; that is, more than three hours into his interrogation the night of March 12, 1994. A hearing was set to review the motion, but, in the meantime, it had thrown the schedule in the case into confusion, and Wallace's trial date had to be postponed.

In April 1995, the court announced its findings. According to the summary of the decision, Wallace was charged before he taped his official Statement of Confession and only after the police felt they had enough suspicion warranting a charge. "At that time," read the statement, the police "advised defendant of his Miranda rights, which defendant said he understood and chose to waive."

The motion also stated that Wallace was "induced" to confessing after he was promised by interrogating detectives to let him visit his girlfriend, Sadie McKnight, and daughter, Kendra. The interrogation team denied any promises had been made and said McKnight's name came up only after Wallace agreed to talk. After her failed attempt to suppress Wallace's confession, Isabel Day looked for a legal avenue to help save Wallace from death.

The case crawled through the court system toward a trial date. On January 27, 1995, Wallace's defense lawyers argued in court that "widespread, unprecedented (sic) and inflammatory publicity would prevent a fair trial in Mecklenburg County or surrounding counties." Wallace's defense wanted to move Wallace's trial to Guilford County, Durham County, or Scotland County. The defense, however, lost the bid to move the trial.

Prosecutor Marsha Goodenow argued against the move. She challenged the results of a June 1994 public opinion poll commissioned by the defense and asked Judge Johnston to consider the impact on victims' families of moving the trial away from Mecklenburg County.

At a preliminary hearing between March 28 and April 6, 1995, Superior Court Judge Robert Johnston heard Wallace's taped confession. The judge had to decide whether jurors could hear the tapes at Wallace's trial. Wallace's defense argued that the confession should be thrown out because police obtained it illegally. Wallace's defense attorneys not only asked Judge Johnson to bar the media and the public from the trial, but also wanted the Judge to order participants in the trial not to talk to reporters and to seal the transcripts until jurors were selected.

On April 20, after lawyers for several news organizations objected to closing the hearing where the tapes of the Wallace interrogation would be played, Judge Johnston made his decision. He ruled that the police took reasonable action and did not violate the constitution when interrogating Wallace after his arrest. He further ruled that neither information released by the CMPD nor media accounts of the crime would prevent Wallace from receiving a fair trial in Mecklenburg County.

Then on November 1, 1995, Judge Johnston denied requests from both sides of the Wallace case to combine nine out of the ten murders in one trial. The lawyers said separate trials would run up costs and delay resolution of the case for more than a year.

On February 6, 1996, Judge Johnston approved a plan to cut the number of charges against Wallace from 34 to 27. Lawyers from both sides agreed that nine murder cases could be tried together "without risk of substantial confusion to the jury." Wallace defense lawyers agreed with the prosecution to have the cases joined in one trial.

On May 7, 1996, Wallace's lawyers revealed that they would use expert testimony about Wallace's mental state at the time of the killings. However, they would not use an insanity defense, which could result in a non-guilty verdict that would eventually set Wallace free.

Finally, on August 27, 1996, Judge Johnston set September 30, 1996, as the trial's starting date. The state would seek the death penalty. Henry Louis Wallace would have his day in court for the brutal murders of nine Charlotte women.

TEN

The Trial

The trial of Henry Louis Wallace took nearly two years to begin, as it was delayed over DNA evidence, choice of venue, and jury selection. Henry Louis Wallace was on trial for the murders of Caroline Love, Shawna Hawk, Audrey Ann Spain, Valencia M. Jumper, Michelle Stinson, Vanessa Little Mack, Betty Jean Baucom, Brandi June Henderson, and Debra Slaughter.

First-degree murder was the only crime that Wallace could be convicted of that was punishable by death. Second-degree murder carries a maximum sentence of life, or fifty years in prison. The defense was hoping for a second-degree murder verdict that would spare Wallace's life.

The prosecution decided not to prosecute Wallace for Sharon Nance's murder because her murder did not fit the pattern of the murders and might do harm to the prosecution's overall case. "The Nance family was hurt because Sharon's name was not included in the court case, and her name was not mentioned in court," said Garry McFadden, who headed the CMPD investigation of Wallace.

For the past eleven months prior to his trial, Wallace had been locked up in Central Prison in Raleigh next to death row for at least eight hours a day in a 12-by-6-foot concrete cell with its only features being a bed, sink, commode, wall locker, and a slit in the window. In continuous service since

1884, Central Prison serves as the admission point into prison for adult male felons sentenced to twenty years or more and is the main medical and mental health center for male offenders. In November 1995, a judge had ordered Wallace be moved to Central Prison for his own protection and away from possible abuses from other inmates.

Central Prison is a close custody facility, which is the highest custody level of North Carolina prisons. Close custody means inmates are closely watched, have high restrictions in their movement, and are under constant armed supervision. Offenders at Central Prison have committed very serious crimes, or present a serious risk to management and refuse to follow rules. As of February 2023, Central Prison houses 752 adult male offenders who are secured by two razor ribbon wire fences.

Wallace was put in isolation under suicide watch and on anti-depressant and anti-psychotic drugs. Wallace spent much of his day playing cards and chatting with other inmates. He was only allowed one, one-hour visit every seven days. Each week, Wallace had just two, one-hour exercise periods outside his cell, which helped to explain how Wallace had gained nearly 100 pounds during his incarceration.

Wallace talked with his defense attorney Isabel Day nearly every week. In explaining how Wallace was doing, Day said: "He has all the time to think about what happened. It's very frightening. He fears the unknown. He's coming to terms with his conscience. As much as anything, he's trying to understand himself and trying to understand what happened."

In August 1996, one month prior to going to trial, Wallace's defense attorneys suffered a setback when Mecklenburg Superior Court Judge Robert Johnston denied the defense's motion to declare the death penalty unconstitutional. Wallace's defense attorneys wanted potential jurors told that if Wallace was sentenced to consecutive life terms, he would never get out of prison. They hoped that the argument would persuade jurors to spare Wallace's life if he was convicted of murder. Day also accused the district attorney's office of being arbitrary in which suspected killers were tried on first-degree murder charges and faced the death penalty. Judge Johnston did not give any reasons for his decision.

Then about five days after Judge Johnston's decision, Wallace's lawyers made a stunning revelation. They claimed that Wallace had been a police informant who had provided police with valuable information about some armed robberies. This had helped police solve some crimes. The defense refused to say if Wallace was an informant during the two-year period that he murdered the ten women. The press speculated that Wallace's defense might be using the information in an attempt to get the jury to spare Wallace's life.

Despite all the maneuvering, the trial began as scheduled on September 30, 1996, with the beginning of jury selection. Veteran prosecutor Marsha Goodenow would be the lead attorney for the State. Goodenow was admitted to the bar in 1984, and prior to her joining the Mecklenburg district attorney's office in 1990, she was both a prosecutor and a defense attorney in the Air Force. Goodenow had earned a reputation as a tough prosecutor who had several wins that included Demeatrius Montgomery, who killed two Charlotte-Mecklenburg police officers; banker David Crespi, who killed his children; and now serial killer Henry Wallace. Goodenow had asked to be assigned to the Wallace case the day after Wallace was charged in March 1994.

Assisting Goodenow was Anne Tompkins, another experienced, no-nonsense prosecutor who had been in that position since 1992. She was assigned to the Wallace case in June 1996. The judge in the case would be 49-year-old Robert Johnston, a Stanford law school graduate who had been a judge since 1982. Colleagues of the judge and the attorneys in the case were confident the trial was in competent hands.

In opening arguments, Goodenow argued for the death penalty, while defense attorney Isabel Day countered that Wallace had suffered from mental illness and that the killings were not first-degree murder because they did not result from "premeditation and deliberation."

On the second day of trial, the Wallace defense made motions to move the trial and to limit DNA testimony. The defense still contended that Wallace could not get a fair trial in Charlotte because of the intense media attention. It also asked the judge to limit expert testimony about DNA tests on semen samples taken from the crime scenes. Judge Johnston recessed court before lunch to consider the motion to move the trial, and he deferred a ruling about the DNA tests.

On October 4, jury selection got under way. Thirty-six prospective jurors were summoned to court and told that the trial would last through Thanksgiving. A guilty verdict on charges of first-degree murder would set up a second process whereby they would decide whether Wallace would live or die.

Attorneys from both sides asked prospective jurors if they could set aside whatever they may know about the case and base their verdict only on the evidence. Some of the prospective jurors told the court they could not.

Day asked one man: "Would it be difficult for you to consider life?"

The man replied: "Yes. I think I have a strong feeling about the death penalty knowing what I know. My natural inclination is that the death penalty is what I feel in my heart if appropriate."

The man was excused from jury service as were thirty-five other prospective jurors. The press surmised that the jury selection process could last several more weeks. On October 7, jury selection resumed.

There was speculation that Wallace could waive his right to a trial and plead guilty to first-degree murder. Legal experts, however, said the process was little used, and given the uncertainty, it could backfire and result in the jury recommending the death penalty. Robert Rosen, a professor of at University of North Carolina at Chapel Hill School of Law who had tried criminal cases, told the *Charlotte Observer*, "I would be reluctant to do it unless there were very strong reasons."

Jury selection dragged on as the lawyers quizzed prospective jurors looking for bias or life experiences that could influence a juror's verdict. Police officers would be called as witnesses, so prosecutors asked prospective jurors about their experiences with law enforcement.

Some of the questions posed to prospective jurists were routine. "Who is your fiancé's boss?" "What did you study in college?" "How long has your brother-in-law been a police officer?" "Do you have a favorite Bible verse?"

Other questions were more personal. "How often do you speak with your Alcoholics Anonymous sponsor?" "What medication do you take for your clinical depression?"

By October 18, 1996, six jurors had been selected from dozens of prospects. Lawyers had to agree on a panel of twelve jurors plus six alternates. The press agreed that the prospective jurists were cooperative and agreeable. Henry Wallace was in court during the jury selection process and conferred with his lawyers when a selection was made.

By mid-November 1996, the lawyers were prepared to give their opening statements in the Wallace trial when Wallace began complaining about painful stomach cramps. Wallace was examined by a jail nurse who gave him Maalox. Wallace was taken to a private doctor who found nothing suspicious, but the doctor suggested further tests. Wallace returned to court the same day. Sheriff's deputies were transferring him under guard to and from the Mecklenburg County jail to the courtroom.

Wallace now weighed more than 300 pounds, having gained more than a hundred pounds between his arrest on March 12, 1994, and the first day of trial, September 30, 1996. Wallace's lawyers blamed the excessive weight gain on inactivity, poor prison food, and a combination of anti-psychotic and anti-depressant drugs.

By November 20, 1996, the court had spent nearly seven weeks selecting twelve jurors and six alternates. The jury included five white women, two Black women, and five white men. All six alternate jurors were white women. The big problem getting jurors to serve was the money it would cost people to serve on the jury, given the time that the trial was supposed to last. The State of North Carolina paid jurors $12 a day for the first week, $30 a day for subsequent weeks—not enough money to replace regular income.

Many of the prospective jurors would find it difficult to serve in a trial expected to be as long as the Wallace trial because their employers limited pay for jury service. North Carolina was typical of the states. Professor Robert Mosteller, a professor at Duke University and an adviser to the North Carolina commission studying court reform, told the *Charlotte Observer* that no state was able to pay jurors what it would take to support a family during a lengthy trial. So, when Judge Johnston asked prospective jurors if serving on a long trial would create personal hardship for them, many said yes.

On November 21, 1996, in her opening statement, Prosecutor Marsha Goodenow told the jury that they should focus on the victims and how the victims had died brutally by stabbings, strangulations, being submerged in a bathtub and doused with rum and set on fire. The victims all had several things in common, Goodenow pointed out, "They were African American women, all young, all very attractive. They all knew the defendant and they all died at his hands. The State is not going to call a single person to that witness stand who saw these murders. We're going to play a tape—the defendant's own voice—telling you everything I just told you."

Defense attorney Isabel Day portrayed Wallace as a victim, a man who was driven by hideous fantasies and disabled by mental illness rooted in his childhood. "For those of you who think he's some kind of monster, this may be hard for you, because I'm going to ask you to look into a monster's mind," Day said.

Meanwhile, as the trial proceeded outside the courtroom, relations between the Charlotte police and the Black community remained volatile. On November 21, at a three-hour Charlotte-Mecklenburg NAACP meeting, several hundred people demanded to know if CMPD officer Michael Marlowe would be charged in the shooting death of 19-year-old James Willie Cooper, an unarmed Black motorist. Deputy Police Chief Glen Mowray told the angry gathering that Officer Marlowe had to make a split-second decision and that the district attorney would make the decision whether to prosecute Marlow.

These answers did not satisfy the gathering, but another meeting was scheduled to discuss the matter further. Meanwhile, several civil rights activists called for the formation of a citizen's review board, as well as an independent investigation of the Cooper shooting.

Back at the Wallace trial, witnesses began to testify. Lamar "Squeaky" Woods, the boyfriend of Wallace murder victim Brandi Henderson, testified how he had come home to find his 10-month-old son Tyrese choking and Henderson lying face down on a bed. Tyrese was in the courtroom with his father, sleeping on a courtroom bench while his father testified. Woods described how when police asked him whom Henderson would have trusted to let in her apartment, he gave the police only three names, one of which was Henry Wallace.

The same day at trial, Lovey Slaughter, the mother of murder victim Deborah Slaughter, took the stand and described how she found her daughter. Lovey and her husband had been sharing the apartment with Deborah, but had moved out a month earlier. Before moving, she had taken a photo from the wall that she had wanted copied and was returning it the day of the murder. Lovey found her daughter lying on the living room floor. She called out "Deborah," but her daughter did not move.

In an interview after her testimony, Lovey talked about how difficult it was to testify and to recall the events of her daughter's murder. "This is very hard," she explained. "We had just started to heal, and this was opening everything back up again. Now the case is underway, and although nothing can be done to bring my daughter back, something needs to be done with the person responsible."

The trial stalled amid motions to move the trial and to limit DNA testimony. Defense lawyers were still claiming that Wallace could not get a fair trial in Mecklenburg County because of the media attention. The defense filed a couple of other motions; namely, one to prevent Mecklenburg's sheriff's deputies and Charlotte-Mecklenburg police from speaking about Wallace or the case against him, and its own request to have a police escort to view the apartment where the women were murdered.

Judge Johnston decided to keep the case in Charlotte. He also denied a defense request to halt police and sheriff's deputies from talking to reporters about Wallace or the case and refused to order a police escort for defense lawyers who wanted to inspect the apartments where the women were killed.

On December 3, 1996, there was testimony about the murder of two of the victims: Audrey Spain and Valencia Jumper. The jury heard the taped confession of Wallace describing how he strangled Spain and how, after strangling Jumper, he deliberately set fire to her place to cover up the crime.

The evidence against Wallace mounted as more witnesses took the stand. Jurors heard testimony ranging from clinical findings of police technicians to Wallace's accounts of the killings. Barbara Rippy struggled as she told how she had found Vanessa Mack's body that Sunday morning. Rippy's son is the father of Vanessa Mack's oldest daughter, Natara, who was seven when her mother was murdered.

After her emotional testimony, Rippy left the courtroom in tears. Following Mack's death, she had moved to Florida, where the children lived with her. Rippy told the court: "Vanessa asked me to raise her children if anything ever happened to her."

By December 7, 1996, the court was nearing the end of the evidence phase of the trial. Jurors had heard ten days of testimony that included more than sixty witnesses and reviewed more than 240 pieces of evidence of photos, lab reports, and ATM bank records. The court now struggled through a presentation that included an overhead projector and various charts. The presentation resembled a university lecture. The presenter was Michael Deguglielmo, a forensic chemist and DNA expert from Nashville, Tennessee. The jurors took notes for several hours, as Deguglielmo compared Wallace's known DNA profile and the DNA in the semen samples from the victims' panties, bed sheets, and blankets.

The jury heard Wallace's disturbing confession. Prosecutors wanted to show that Wallace had formed a specific intent to kill, an element they needed to prove first-degree murder. The defense, on the other hand, was trying to prove that Wallace was mentally ill and this made him incapable of intent. At stake—the death penalty.

The jury took notes from reviewing the transcript of Wallace's interview with police investigators. Prosecutors played the tape in which Wallace stated his intent when he went to Brandi Henderson's apartment.

"Why did you go to the apartment?" an investigator asked Wallace.

"Robbery and murder," was the answer.

Four days later, the defense presented one of its most important witnesses: Robert Ressler, a paid consultant and former head of the FBI's violent criminal apprehension unit. In early 1994, police had asked the FBI for help, but the FBI said, after examining the Charlotte murders, that they were not the work of a serial killer.

The defense wanted Ressler to corroborate a psychologist's testimony that Wallace was mentally ill and incapable of forming a specific intent to kill. If the jury found Ressler's testimony credible, Wallace would not be convicted of first-degree murder and thus would not face the death penalty.

Prosecutor Goodenow aggressively questioned Ressler's expertise and challenged the admissibility of his testimony. Ressler said his testimony was based on a wealth of credible evidence that included several hours of interviews with Wallace, as well as photos, autopsy reports, and information from the police.

Wallace may have created a new type of serial killer, Ressler told the court. For one thing, Wallace knew all of the victims. "An acquaintance serial killer...I think we're talking about the first one," Ressler told the court. "The hallmark of a serial killer is selecting victims he can distance himself from."

In comparing Wallace to other serial killers he has studied, Ressler testified that Wallace showed signs of what he described as both "organized" and "disorganized" behavior. Ressler explained that those of mixed category behavior tend to be mentally ill. He said, in researching the case, he reached the conclusion that Wallace was also mentally ill and like other similar serial killers, Ressler revealed, Wallace was troubled by pangs of conscience. "Like Mr. Wallace said, your life becomes very disjointed, you're very paranoid, you feel the police are coming to your door," Ressler testified.

Many of the relatives of Wallace's victims were in the courtroom day in and day out listening to the lawyers present or try to refute the evidence in the case. Wallace sat a few feet away, but Lovey and her husband, Alphonso, aware of Wallace's presence, would look straight ahead.

The testimony was especially excruciating when Wallace's confession on tape was playing and he described the events surrounding their loved one's death. Lovey Slaughter bowed her head and read the Bible, especially Psalms 35 and 121.

Henry Wallace on tape: "…and I told her to give me everything that was in her purse. And she pulled out the money, which was about $40…And then I tightened the towel very tightly, and she fell to the floor and she started kicking." Lovey Slaughter listened, then bowed her head and read her Bible.

On December 12, 1996, prosecutors put James M. Sullivan, the medical examiner, on the stand to testify about the cause of death for each of the nine women Wallace was charged with killing. Sullivan told the court that two of the women died from stab wounds and seven from strangulation. He said none of the victims showed physical evidence of genital injuries. Sullivan held up graphic photos for the jury to see and pointed out the wounds. Michelle Stinson had four stab wounds and Deborah Slaughter, thirty-eight.

On cross examination, defense lawyer Jim Cooney emphasized Sullivan's conclusion about the absence of genital injuries. Wallace had pled not guilty to nine counts of first-degree rape. His lawyers were hoping to spare Wallace the death penalty by arguing that the women were not raped.

The prosecution by now had called more than sixty witnesses. The following day, the defense called their expert witness, Ann Burgess, professor of psychiatric nursing at the

University of Pennsylvania, to counter the State's evidence about how he killed the nine women and why. The defense's plan was to keep Wallace off death row by trying to prove that he was mentally ill and could not form the intent to kill, the key element required to make the murder punishable by death. In all, the defense called three witnesses to testify.

Burgess presented a bleak picture of Wallace growing up, the 400-square-foot house with no indoor plumbing, beatings by the mother, being paraded around the neighborhood in women's clothes. She testified how his anger and resentment toward Black women who dominated him fueled fantasies that put him in control and led to murder. Burgess said Wallace suffered from a personality disorder with eight components, including paranoia, narcissism, and obsessive-compulsive disorder.

A second witness, Robert Sadoff, a psychiatrist from the University of Pennsylvania, agreed with Burgess, saying Wallace was capable at some points of forming the intent to kill, which is clearly expressed in the confession.

Goodenow challenged the admissibility of the experts' testimony, saying it was based on hearsay from Wallace. Wallace was being charged with rape as well as murder, but Burgess said she did not believe the rapes occurred.

Defense attorney Cooney asked Burgess, "Is the evidence consistent with Wallace's claims of rape and murder?" Burgess said no and cited the lack of genital trauma and the fact that most of the women were found fully clothed. The sight of seeing a woman who had been raped and strangled was traumatic, Burgess told jurors. This led to signs of mental illness showing up when Wallace was an adolescent. Given that he suffered from a mixed personality disorder, he was incapable of forming a specific intent to kill.

This argument was crucial to the prosecution's goal to get a death penalty verdict for Wallace's crimes. If the jury agreed with the defense, Wallace would not receive a first-degree murder verdict and he would be spared the death penalty.

Did she interview any of Wallace's sex partners? His ex-wife? His former girlfriend? Prosecutor Goodenow asked Burgess. Burgess said no. Goodenow revealed she was prepared to call a rebuttal witness, a woman from South Carolina whom Wallace had raped and who would testify that Wallace's "sexual functioning is fine."

Both Burgess and Sadoff were paid well for their consulting. They each received $100 an hour. Burgess had received about $10,000 for her role in the case up until the time of her testimony.

On December 12, the prosecution rested its case against Wallace. Wallace's defense attorneys began presenting their case by interviewing experts outside the presence of the jury.

Robert Ressler, former head of the FBI's Violence criminal apprehension unit was back for the defense. He revealed that he had spent six to seven hours interviewing Wallace. In testifying, Ressler said about Wallace: "If, in fact, (Wallace) elected to be a serial killer, he was going about it in all the wrong ways."

Ressler discussed his "organized" and "disorganized" categories of serial killers, placing Wallace into a "mixed" category with attributes of both. Ressler described Wallace's crimes as "sexual homicides" and said it was greatly influenced by true detective magazines with their depiction of provocatively dressed women in distress, feeding fantasies of domination and control.

Hammering home the case for not giving Wallace the death penalty, defense witness Ann Burgess contended that Wallace suffered from mental illness when he committed the murders. She backed up Ressler's contention that Wallace suffered from mixed personality disorder, describing Wallace's personality as being "with a lot of holes in it—like Swiss cheese." She added that "a lot of social conditions—

absence of a father, childhood sexual exploitation, beatings from his mother, for example—contributed to his mental illness and helped impair his ability to form intent." Burgess said Wallace gave the best evidence of his mental illness in his police confession when he described the murders of Shawna Hawk, Aubrey Spain, Caroline Love, and Valencia Jumper.

As the trial wound down, testimony focused on Wallace's fascination as a child with true detective magazines. Ann Burgess, testifying for the defense, said Wallace got access to the magazines through his mother, who was a devoted reader of them. Robert Ressler, also testified for the defense, saying, "He was certainly caught up in this kind of literature. He probably picked up a lot of ideas." Ressler said the kind of stilted language that Wallace used in confessing his crimes—"I performed sex on," "I administered the choke hold (sic)"—may have come from the true detective magazines.

Ressler revealed that thirty-six of the serial killers he interviewed for a study reported an interest in the magazine genre. Criminologists, however, say that most readers of true detective magazines are not dangerous or violent. However, for people prone to violence, it can spur in some readers fantasies that lead to violence.

Burgess and Ressler had testified for three and a half grueling days. With the end of their testimony, the prosecution opted not to call any rebuttal witnesses. The defense also rested without calling another witness to testify. Wallace waived his right to testify leaving jurors with his words in the taped confession he had made to police on March 12, 1994. Closing arguments were scheduled for December 30, 1994, the day the jurors returned from the holidays. The court was inching toward a verdict.

ELEVEN

The Verdict

The jury of twelve and its six alternates began deliberating Henry Louis Wallace's fate on January 2, 1997, but deliberations were delayed after one of the jurors reported a death in his wife's family. When it was learned the funeral would be held Friday of the following week, lawyers from both sides agreed that deliberations would be over by then.

Wallace was on trial accused of the rape and murder of nine Charlotte women in what had become the biggest murder prosecution in North Carolina history. The jurors had received nearly four hours of legal instructions from Mecklenburg Superior Court Judge Robert Johnston.

The jurors' task of determining a verdict was complicated. A guilty verdict for Wallace on any of the nine murder charges against him would require a separate sentencing hearing to decide whether he should be executed. Jurors had to reach unanimous verdicts on each of the twenty-eight charges against Wallace, which included nine counts of first-degree murder, eight counts of first-degree rape, one count of second-degree rape, five robberies, four offenses involving forced oral sex, and one assault on the infant son of murder victim, Brandi Henderson. Defense lawyers acknowledged that Wallace murdered the nine women, but contended that Wallace lacked the mental capacity to form the specific intent to kill, which is required to make execution an option.

The jurors elected a foreman, a 42-year-old corporate advertising executive, one of two college graduates on the jury. Given the complex nature of the case, transcripts in all nine killings were sent to the jurors. They could also ask to review any of the exhibits introduced during the five-week trial.

By January 7, 1997, the jury had deliberated thirteen hours over three days. They had heard the taped confessions of Wallace and reviewed the transcripts. They asked for and reviewed photographs of Tyrese Woods, the ten-month old son of Brandi Henderson, Wallace's eighth victim. Wallace was charged with choking the child after raping and murdering his mother.

The trial had taken four months, and there were 400 exhibits, 75 witnesses, and seven hours of confession heard by the jury. Experts had billed for more than $100,000 for evaluating Wallace. Lawyers had worked hundreds of hours through Thanksgiving, Christmas, and New Year's. The trial had taken its toll on victim family members who had the will to attend the trial. For example, after their first trips to court, two family members were hospitalized: one for high blood pressure, the other for emotional distress.

And now the jury was ready to announce its decision. When the jury came back from deliberating, they found Henry Wallace guilty of nine counts of first-degree murder, according to the Appellate Report, "each on the basis of malice, premeditation (sic) and deliberation." In addition, the jury found the defendant guilty of eight counts of first-degree rape, one count of second-degree rape, two counts of first-degree sexual offense, two counts of sexual offense, one count of assault with a deadly weapon, one count of assault on a child under the age of twelve (sic) and five counts of robbery with a dangerous weapon. In all, Wallace was convicted of twenty-nine crimes in his nearly two-year killing spree that began with the murder of Caroline Love on June 15, 1992, and ended with his arrest on March 12, 1994.

To save Wallace's life, his defense lawyers called character witnesses to present mitigating factors such as mental illness and abuses Wallace faced as a child. In all, the defense called six character witnesses, including a minister and Wallace's cheerleading sponsor at Barnwell High, and showed three others on videotape. The court heard five days of testimony in the sentencing phase of the trial. The prosecution did not call any new witnesses, but they argued that the way Wallace killed and the fact that rape, robberies, and other felonies were committed during the killings, the death penalty was warranted.

Charlotte psychologist Faye Sultan contended that Wallace did not have a complete personality. She diagnosed Wallace as having aspects of a half-dozen personality disturbances, including depression, narcissism, dependence, paranoia, and obsessive-compulsive disorder.

Another defense witness, New York social worker Carmeta Albarus, suggested that Wallace's mother, Lottie Mae Wallace, was the root cause of his problems by restricting his activities and "projecting (on her son) her feelings of rage toward the men who caused her pain." Lottie Mae never attended the trial and refused to talk to reporters.

Prosecutor Goodenow challenged Albarus's testimony, stating that if Wallace's defense wanted to use information about Wallace, they should put his mother on the witness stand and not rely on hearsay testimony. Goodenow asked Albarus how restrictive was Wallace's mother? After all, he belonged to his high school's 4-H Club, was on the Vocational Student Council, and was a cheerleader and a photographer for the student newspaper. Goodenow asked Albarus if she had talked to Wallace about the nine women he murdered. "Did you ask him if he said, as he strangled these women, 'Hurry up and die bitch, I hate you, you sorry son of a bitch'?" Goodenow asked. Albarus answered: "What he said was, those are the same words his mother used on him."

The sentencing phase ended with the testimony of a reluctant witness: Sadie McKnight, Wallace's former girlfriend. She was the only rebuttal witness called by the State. McKnight was called by the prosecution over the vigorous objections of Wallace's lawyers. McKnight had dated Wallace for nearly two years and had broken up with him about a month before he was arrested.

In a hostile cross-examination, Isabel Day asked McKnight: "Why did you stay?"

McKnight's answer: "Because he'll deceive you into thinking he's one thing and he's not. I learned that the hard way. There are people out there grieving, and I've got to live with that."

McKnight described Wallace's mother as a "normal woman" and "nice lady" who did not yell at her son. She said she never saw Wallace's mother act inappropriately, nor did she have pornography in the house.

Defense attorney Day challenged McKnight aggressively, questioning her motives for testifying against Wallace. Day asked McKnight three times: "Do you want Henry dead?"

McKnight's picture of Wallace's mother was contradicted by Aleah Thomas Cole, another girlfriend, who described Mrs. Wallace as "a nasty, hypocritical person." Cole had started dating Wallace after his marriage broke up in 1989. Wallace, Cole said, would talk to her about problems he had with his mother and wife. Cole acknowledged that she had given a different version of her breakup with Wallace to the defense.

As the sentencing phase of the trial drew to the close, jurors had heard a lot of contradictory evidence. It would be a challenging task for the jury to reach a unanimous verdict.

If it could not do that, Wallace would not get the death penalty, but would spend the rest of his life in prison. The lawyers faced the jury one last time on January 19, 1997, to make their case as to whether Wallace should live or die.

Prosecutor Goodenow portrayed Wallace as a heartless predator who not only murdered friends who trusted him, but enjoyed their suffering. "I can hear them begging me. I love to hear that. I love to be in power," said Goodenow, quoting Wallace's own words. The prosecution downplayed the defense's emotional arguments, saying that the defense talked a lot about mercy, but Wallace had not shown mercy to his victims. "If ever compelling facts exist to justify imposition of the death penalty, they exist here," Goodenow told the jury. "Don't be the last people who were manipulated and deceived by this defendant."

Isabel Day was emotional as she made a last plea to spare Henry Wallace's life. "I stand before you to beg—beg for the life of Henry Wallace. I say I'm standing, but I'm really kneeling before you, because I know the power you have over the man I've come to know in the last three years." As she spoke, Day held photos of Wallace's wretched life as a child in the run-down house that served as home. Defense attorney Cooney argued, "Putting him to death is not going to erase the grief of those families and bring those victims back, or if I could, I'd strap him to the chair myself."

On January 19, the verdict in the Henry Wallace trial was handed down. The jury agreed with the prosecution's argument that aggravating circumstances outweighed mitigating circumstances. They gave Wallace nine death sentences, one to each of the women he admitted to raping and killing. Judge Robert Johnston read aloud the recommendations for the death penalty nine times, each time ending the sentencing with, "May God have mercy on your soul." Johnston added ten consecutive life sentences and 322 years in prison for twenty other convictions. Defense lawyer Isabel Day wept after the trial ended, not for her court loss, but because the emotion she needed to control over the months of trial could finally be released.

In hearing the verdict, Wallace removed his glasses and wiped his eyes. As he rose from the defense table, ten armed deputies, situated around the courtroom, stood up. Family members gasped in horror at the sight of serial killer Wallace standing before them. Normally, defendants in murder trials are not allowed to address the courtroom, but Judge Johnston allowed it because Wallace was sentenced for other crimes.

Nobody in the courtroom expected Wallace to make a speech. There was dead silence as Wallace spoke. "What words, in any language, can I say that will bring you comfort, quiet the storm, or release you from the mental prison I have put you in? I'm sorry? I apologize? I didn't mean to do it? I guess that all these words, and all that I know, fall far short of what's needed to console any of you.

"Please remember from the Book of Mark 11:25-26," Wallace told the court. Then he read from a three-page statement: "And when you start praying, forgive, if you have nothing against anyone, then your Father also which is heaven forgive your trespasses."

One woman could not help herself, and she lunged at Wallace, only to be restrained by deputies. A man shouted: "Why did you kill them?" Then he collapsed, the sound of his sobs filling the court room.

Family members were shocked and disgusted by Wallace's speech. "I was outraged, appalled," Dee Sumpter, the mother of murder victim Shawna Hawk, said. Other victims' family members spoke up. Alphonse and Lovey Slaughter said they forgave Wallace. "If his pleas for forgiveness are sincere, I know God will forgive him," Lovey Slaughter told the *Charlotte Observer*. "I will pray for his soul that God will forgive him." But the Slaughters doubted Wallace was sincere.

George Burrell, the cousin of Brandi Henderson, said he could forgive Wallace because that is the way he was raised, but added, "I'll never know why my cousin or any of the other girls had to die." Kathy Love, victim Caroline Love's sister, looked pleased at the verdict, but then charged toward Wallace and had to be restrained. She later apologized for her action, saying it would be hard to forgive Wallace, but she knew it was something she would have to do.

Venus Herron, the sister of Sharon Nance, Wallace's first victim in Charlotte, was in the courtroom, even though Wallace was not tried for Sharon's murder. Nance's murder was not tried because it did not fit the pattern of the case. For one thing, Wallace knew the other nine victims. Wallace claimed Nance was a prostitute and after consensual sex killed her when she asked for money. Family members denied Sharon Nance was a prostitute, but even if she was, they argued, it was no reason to kill her. Wallace also admitted to killing Tashanda Bethea in Barnwell and authorities were still deciding what to do with that murder.

Meanwhile, Henry Louis Wallace was taken from the Mecklenburg courthouse to a 67-square-foot cell on death row at Central Prison in Raleigh, North Carolina, to await execution. Death sentences are automatically appealed to the North Carolina Supreme Court, but it looked like it was only a matter of time before Wallace would pay for his crimes with his life.

TWELVE

The Aftermath

After his conviction, Henry Wallace, North Carolina's most prolific serial killer, joined 160 men and three women on death row. North Carolina's death row population had reached an all-time high since the state took over executions in 1910, steadily increasing since 1977 when the death penalty was reinstated. In the thirteen years from 1977 through 1989, an average of ten killers was sentenced to death each year in North Carolina. Between 1990 and 1997, a total of 143 death sentences were handed down, an average of about twenty a year, although no one was executed in 1996. North Carolina's death row population was the sixth-highest among the thirty-eight states that had the death penalty.

North Carolina reflected a national trend. Death sentences in the U.S. had risen every year in the 1990s. Across the country, more than 3,100 men and women were on death row.

Henry Wallace arrived at Central Prison at 6:10 p.m. on January 29, 1997, where he was immediately taken to the prison hospital for medical and psychological screening. Three hours later, at 9:47 p.m., Wallace was in his cell on death row. Wallace shared a double bunk in a 12-foot by 4-foot cell because the burgeoning death row population had forced prison officials to put condemned killers in the double bunks in day rooms near the single cells. Prison officials said Wallace would get a cell to himself when one became available. It could be quite a wait, though, since seventeen prisoners were in line for a cell before him.

Wallace's day began at 6 a.m. when prison officials counted heads. He got one hour a day for exercise and could shower twice a week. Wallace was allowed to go to an outdoor exercise area twice a week where he could walk, jog, or play basketball. Wallace could not accept calls. In fact, he could receive only one call per year.

Wallace was allowed one visit a week where inmates could see and talk with their visitors, but could not have any physical contact. Most of the visits to see Wallace came from Rebecca Torrijas, a prison psychiatric nurse whom Wallace married on June 5, 1998. Blond and fragile looking, Torrijas is a white woman twenty-three years Wallace's senior, although observers at the time noted that she looked younger than her age. Torrijas told the press she had been fired after her employer saw her at a televised hearing regarding Wallace in 1995. Torrijas was a constant presence at Wallace's trial.

For her wedding with Wallace, Torrijas was described as wearing a pale green dress with pink flowers and a pearl necklace. Wallace wore his red prison jump suit and black tennis shoes. Isabel Day, Wallace's co-trial lawyer, served as an official witness and photographer for the marriage. Also attending was the manager of the Death Row unit at the prison.

The newlyweds were allowed to talk with each other for about twenty minutes in the room where they were married. Afterward, they were united in another room where, separated by bars and plastic glass, they chatted for about an hour.

To bring a sense of closure for the families of Wallace's victims, a prayer service was held at Gethesemane Baptist Church on February 2, 1997. Lights were dimmed as family members and friends, numbering nearly a hundred, lit candles honoring each of Wallace's victims: Caroline Love, age 20; Shawna Hawk, 20; Audrey Spain, 24; Valencia Jumper, 21; Michelle Stinson, 20; Vanessa Mack, 25; Betty Baucom, 18; and Deborah Slaughter, 35. The memorial also honored Sharon Nance and Tashanda Bethea, the two other women Wallace was charged with killing.

Jury members also attended the memorial. There were a lot of tears, as family members read poems and spoke tributes. Dee Sumpter told the gathering, "You are a part of a very special thing. Because of this, you now know better how to love."

Soon after Wallace's conviction and sentencing, Wallace's new defense team of Thomas Maher and Ann Petersen, appointed to represent Wallace on December 28, 2000, began working for a new trial. They argued that Wallace deserved a new trial because prosecutors misled jurors and withheld evidence that might have persuaded jurors to sentence him to life in prison. They acknowledged Wallace committed the killings, but argued that mental illness and drug addiction kept Wallace from premeditating the murders. Wallace's lawyers also accused the prosecution of failing to turn over to the defense tapes and handwritten notes from witness interviews that could have helped save Wallace's life.

State prosecutors called Wallace's claims meritless and contended that he had received a fair trial. No evidence was withheld, the State argued. "Defendant contention that the verdict of guilty to first-degree murder would have been different does not pass the 'straight face' test," argued Steven Arbogast, North Carolina's Special Deputy Attorney General. "There is no reasonable probability of a different sentence for the murder of nine women."

Wallace also appealed having defense investigator Valerie Woodard assigned to his case. He claimed Woodard was afraid of him and disliked him. In an affidavit, Wallace contended, "I thought Valerie Woodard did not like me because she thinks that if I were out on the street, I would kill her. It was clear to me that Valerie Woodard disliked me, was afraid of me (sic) and biased against me."

The prosecutors dismissed Wallace's charge of bias, stating, "The defendant is not entitled to attorneys or investigators that 'like' him or accept his murderous conduct. Wallace's lawyers had produced no evidence that Woodard's work hurt Wallace's defense."

Woodard felt compelled to challenge Wallace's assertion against her. "I don't think about whether I like him (Wallace) or not," she said. "I had a job to do. And that's what I did."

Wallace filed a direct appeal to the North Carolina Supreme Court challenging his convictions and death sentences. Wallace asserted that due to the extensive pretrial publicity surrounding his case, he was unable to get an impartial jury and fair trial in Mecklenburg County. He claimed that the trial court's refusal to grant his motions for a change of venue deprived him of his Sixth, Eighth, and Fourteen Amendments to the U.S. Constitution.

Wallace also contended that the trial court erred when it denied his motion to suppress his pretrial statements to police. Wallace charged that police investigators deliberately delayed advising him of his Miranda rights in order to gain a confession from him. Wallace claimed that because this delay was deliberate, his subsequent confessions were involuntary.

Wallace also claimed that Valerie Woodard, the investigator hired to assist the defense, rendered ineffective assistance under the Sixth Amendment because she had a conflict of interest. The Supreme Court ruled that Wallace provided no evidence that Woodard was authorized to practice law at the time she worked as an investigator for the defense. Nor did Wallace, the court ruled, provide any evidence that Woodard, if she was authorized to practice law, performed any legal service for him.

The North Carolina Supreme Court affirmed Wallace's conviction on November 27, 2000. Six months later, the U. S. Supreme Court denied Wallace's appeal. The legal battle to save Wallace's life had gone through the state and federal courts. Wallace had languished on North Carolina's Death Row for eight years when Superior Court Judge Charles Lamm rejected Wallace's latest appeal on May 18, 2005.

In a 63-page memorandum, Judge Lamm rejected every one of Wallace's claims, ruling that "the State did not suppress any favorable or impeaching evidence. All of the evidence was available, either from other sources or by the simple device of interviewing the individuals."

The judge also rejected Wallace's claims that his lawyers were ineffective because they didn't remove Woodard as the investigator. He also ruled it constitutional that the court had the authority to sentence him to death. The judge wrote, "The defendant received a fair trial and sentencing hearing, a trial resulting in a verdict worthy of confidence. The State did not hide or conceal any of these individuals from the defense. They were known to the defense."

The rejection was the first in the second round of appeals that was expected to wind through the state and federal courts over the next few years. How long those appeals would take was unknown, but the press noted that, in North Carolina, death row appeals usually took eight to twelve years.

Four Charlotte men have been executed in the twenty-five years between 1978 and 2003. The average time between their initial death sentence and the execution was just under thirteen years. Of the 194 prisoners on North Carolina's death row in the last twenty-five years until 2005, 48 have been there longer than ten years.

In August 2010, Wallace was one of fifteen death row inmates who filed to have their sentences converted to life in prison under North Carolina's Racial Justice Act. The North Carolina Racial Justice Act (RJA) allowed capital defendants to challenge their death sentences if they successfully prove that race was a significant factor in decisions to seek or impose the death penalty at the time of their trials. The law had passed both the Senate and North Carolina House of Representatives and was signed into law by Governor Bev Perdue.

The law, however, came under pressure from a group of forty-three district attorneys, who expressed opposition to the act citing the clog of the court system in the state. The North Carolina Senate passed a bill by a 27-14 vote on November 28, 2011, that would effectively repeal the Racial Justice Act, and the law was repealed in 2013.

Meantime, no execution date has ever been set for Henry Wallace and family members of the victims continue to wait for justice to be done. It has taken its toll on victim family members. Linda Moore, the sister of Wallace's last victim, Deborah Slaughter, revealed that she went into a deep depression after her death and experienced a long period of denial. "It was a shock, devastating," Moore recalled. "We were the only daughters in the family, so Debra (sic) and I were close. She was the first person in our immediate family to die."

In 1984, Moore's father, Alphonso Slaughter, moved his family from Florida to Charlotte, as a result of his work with the Church of God. But, one year after arriving, his job was eliminated. Then through a series of setbacks, his license to preach was revoked. Alphonso struggled financially to stay afloat. He managed to get a job driving a bus for the city.

Alphonso's hard luck continued. His health deteriorated, and then his daughter Deborah's body was discovered. "My whole heart fell out," Alphonso recalled for the *Charlotte Observer.* "The bottom came out of everything."

Alphonso's health crashed as he tried driving a taxi. Blood pressure at stroke level. Sleep apnea. In 1996, triple bypass surgery. Professional help for depression. A psychiatrist who recommended a psychologist.

"Debra's (sic) death was unbearable for my parents, especially for my father," Moore recalled. "I'm sure it contributed to my father's death. And my mother...she has a lot of health issues, but is holding on."

Dee Sumpter has always believed that the police could have done more to bring Henry Wallace to justice more quickly. "For some unknown reason, they just couldn't connect the dots," Sumpter says. "Was there racism? I think so."

Ironically, her feelings toward Garry McFadden, who headed CMPD's Wallace investigation, have mellowed over the years to the point that she and McFadden can now be considered friends. "After Wallace murdered her daughter, Shawna, Dee was very upset with us (the police), and she had a right to be," McFadden recalled. "There was no progress in the investigation, and I can understand that. But she knows I tried, and, over time, we became close friends. We have a great relationship, and I've kept in touch. I communicate with her almost every week."

In 2011, Mothers of Murdered Offspring (MOM-O), the victims support organization started by Sumpter and David Howard and her late friend Judy Williams, gave McFadden and other police officers who worked the Wallace case a banquet and a special award. "It was a real big deal for us officers who worked the Wallace case," McFadden revealed.

MOM-O was formed March 29, 1993, about five weeks after Wallace murdered Sumpter's daughter, Shawna Mack. Organizers were Dee Sumpter, David Howard, and the late Judy Williams. At that time, there were no organizations or support groups dedicated to helping families of murder victims cope with the pain, anger, and the sudden devastation they were forced to endure. MOM-O regularly holds meetings in churches, schools, and community centers and are supported by corporate and private sponsors. In 1993, Mothers of Murdered Offspring was established as a 501(c)3 non-profit organization with a dual mission to support families through the cycle of grief and devastation that murder causes and to create and support programs and activities that focus on violence prevention.

MOM-O's mission, according the statement on its web site is 1) to be the primary resource by which mothers and families of murder victims are supported in the days, weeks, years following the loss of a loved one and directed to resources and information to help them, mentally, emotionally, financially (sic) and spiritually recover; 1a) to be the network by which survivors and the community are brought together to support and encourage one another; 2) to develop new and innovative violence prevention and substance abuse awareness initiatives through youth programs, gun and relationship violence prevention (sic) and anti-drug and substance abuse campaigns and education."

Sumpter has stepped away from the organization, realizing she needed to focus on her own healing, but MOM-O is capably headed today by executive director Lisa Crawford who has not lost anyone to violence but who is dedicated to helping those who have. "As soon as someone is murdered, shortly thereafter we get the report that says 'here's the next-of-kin,'" said Crawford. "Most of them are so devastated that they cannot imagine the tragedy has happened to them. We help them with funeral arrangements, but then we also do candlelight vigils." The support continues after the vigils.

McFadden has done well for himself since leaving his sergeant's job with the Charlotte Metropolitan Police Department (CMPD) to head the Wallace investigation. McFadden readily acknowledges that the Wallace case has had a tremendous impact on his career and how he views police work. "After Wallace, I started looking at cases differently," McFadden revealed. "It encouraged me to do more when I was involved in a homicide investigation. I became a better detective. You got to spend time in the community. You have to listen to the community. You got to be ready to answer questions the community may have. Citizens have talked to me more. They have trusted me more. For me, that's great."

McFadden was sworn in for his second term as the Mecklenburg County sheriff in December 2022, saying he hopes to improve relationships between law enforcement and the communities it serves during his time in office.

The ceremony took place at the Charlotte-Mecklenburg Government Center in Uptown Charlotte. McFadden was first elected as sheriff in 2018. He ran unopposed in the midterm election after winning the Democratic primary in May 2022.

McFadden appeared in a 2018 Investigative Discovery TV special titled *Bad Henry*. It chronicled how McFadden and his homicide unit hunted down and caught serial killer Henry Wallace. The documentary featured interrogation tapes and stories from both investigators and families of Wallace's eleven known victims.

McFadden told *Fox News,* "It's been twenty-five years. I talked to some of the family members. And I'm still getting phone calls from family members as we speak. We thought it was important for the story to be told."

Earlier in 2016, McFadden, who in his thirty-four years with the CMPD investigated more than 800 homicides, ninety percent of which were solved, appeared in his own TV serial show titled *I am Homicide* in which he solved murder cases in Charlotte. In May 2022, he played a central role in ABC's 20/20 documentary, *Lock the Door Behind You,* which reported on the latest developments in the case and featured an exclusive interview with Tyrese Woods, the son of victim Brandi Henderson, whom Wallace had tried to murder when he was ten months old. Woods discussed life today after surviving an attack by Wallace when he was a baby.

The CMPD received much criticism from the Charlotte community for its handling of the Wallace investigation.

Most damning was the charge that the police were less committed to investigating the murders because the victims were young African American women from the working-class area of the city. The police denied that they cared less about the victims, but conceded that their investigative techniques needed examining and refining. In October 1996, the CMPD, while probing the murders of four other women, set up a task to look for similarities with other unsolved cases.

The previous November, the CMPD announced that it would become the first police force in North Carolina to have on-site DNA testing. The CMPD, unlike other North Carolina police departments, did not rely on the State Bureau of Investigation laboratory in Raleigh. Moreover, the move would significantly cut down the time it took to get the results from the State. The Wallace trial was forthcoming and the police wouldn't say whether having a lab would have led them to Wallace being arrested sooner. In a string of crimes, DNA samples can either confirm or rule out that a single suspect is responsible.

"If we have DNA capabilities, we will be able to set our own priorities," CMPD Deputy Police Chief Larry Snider told the press. "We can control the time frame."

In 1994, Dennis Nowicki, the executive director of the Illinois Criminal Justice Information Authority, was chosen to be chief of the CMPD. Nowicki was a thirty-year police veteran, twenty-five of those years with the Chicago police department. Nowicki chose Charlotte over other job possibilities with the police departments of Boston and Buffalo.

In his North Carolina post, Nowicki took over a 1,400-member department with 1,200 sworn police officers. The City of Charlotte and Mecklenburg County merged their departments in October 1993, making it the 28th-largest municipal department in the country. During his first year on the job, Nowicki made changes quickly. There were seven police investigators when he arrived. He increased the number to twenty-one. The number eventually grew to four times larger.

Nowicki also supported the Violent Crime Task Force, which focused on removing the worst offenders from the streets. Over the years, the CMPD has set up several task forces to probe continually for common clues among unsolved murder cases.

Nowicki began making other changes. For one thing, Charlotte police officers would experience more comprehensive training. Officers were already attending classes on how to develop profiles of criminals, while more would be sent to sessions on interrogations soon. Nowicki also planned to give investigators better access to technology as well as upgraded computerized analysis of suspects and cases.

There would be a reduced workload for homicide detectives. To do that, Nowicki planned to increase the number of homicide detectives from fifteen to eighteen. He also planned to take away hit-and-run accident deaths and suicides from the homicide unit.

Nowicki said the CMPD recognized the need for better relations with families of victims. He planned to set up a focus group where families and victims' assistance groups could tell police investigators what the department should do better.

Nowicki talked about policing being a partnership between the police and community. "Crime can't be solved by the police alone," Nowicki told the press. "We have to mobilize the entire community. But we also have to organize our resources, trying to be smarter—making arrests that affect the quality of life."

In May 1994, two months after Nowicki's hiring, CMPD officially adopted Community Problem-Oriented Policing (CPOP) as an operating philosophy, committing itself to working with residents and neighborhood leaders to identify and solve community problems that lead to crime. CPOP is an information intensive strategy that places a premium on data, intelligence, community input, and analysis. The analysis is designed to reveal critical aspects of the problem that can be altered to effect a reduction in the problem. The approach showed signs of working, as overall crime rates began to drop.

Despite the changes, relations between the CMPD and the Charlotte community, especially its Black residents, remained tense. On November 19, 1996, CMPD officer Michael Marlow, a white officer, shot and killed 19-year-old Black motorist James Cooper after Cooper refused to get out of his car during a traffic stop. Cooper's four-year-old daughter was in the back seat. Marlow said he believed Cooper was reaching for a gun. The district attorney did not pursue charges.

Then on April 9, 1997, CMPD officers Shannon Jordan and Donn Belz shot a combined 22 times at a moving car, killing 33-year-old Carolyn Sue Boetticher, a Black woman. Jordan, a white officer, was fired, and Belz, also white, was suspended thirty days before being returned to duty. The department went eleven years without disciplining an officer for an unjustified shooting; that is, until officer Jenny Curlee lost her job for firing into a car on Central Avenue.

By the 2000s, Charlotte's population and economy was exploding, but the growth brought a rise in overall crime, including increased gang activity. Increasingly, city leaders and residents soured on Police Chief Dennis Nowicki's adherence to the CPOP philosophy, which they perceived as too passive in fighting crime. In August 1999, Charlotte hired St. Petersburg, Fla., Police Chief Darrel Stephens to take over for Dennis Nowicki, who had left for a consultant's job.

By 2019, Charlotte was seeing a surge in crime, averaging three murders per week. Dee Sumpter showed up at an event, telling the press, "I can't believe, twenty-six years later, I'm still here. And I'm still making the plea. We can't let this go on in (sic) city that views itself progressive. It's unacceptable."

On May 25, 2020, African American George Floyd was killed by an officer in Minneapolis, Minnesota, during an arrest made after a store clerk suspected Floyd may have used a counterfeit twenty-dollar bill. After Floyd's murder, protests were held in Charlotte against the lack of police accountability and the use of excessive force by police officers against Black suspects. In response to Floyd's killing, in November 2020, Charlotte City Council passed a slate of reforms for the CMPD, the most prominent being the handing off of some calls for service to civilians or trained mental health clinicians.

On June 23, 2021, Charlotte-Mecklenburg Police launched its newest reform initiative, a training program to create more positive interactions between police and the public. The police reform initiative focuses on CMPD's customer experience vision and will encourage officers to show empathy, compassion, and kindness anytime they encounter the public, even if the situation is negative. CMPD chief Johnny Jennings hopes the program and positive encounters between police and the public will change the public's perception of police and lead to stronger relationships.

Calls for police reforms in Charlotte have continued in an effort to hold the police accountable and deal with racial bias within the criminal justice system. Meanwhile, as of this writing, Wallace has remained on death row at Central Prison in Raleigh, North Carolina, for more than twenty-five years, ironically acting as a catalyst for police reform.

The date for Wallace's execution is still not determined. North Carolina has had a moratorium, that is, a temporary halt on executions since the early 2000's. When and will that moratorium be lifted? As Sheriff McFadden responded when posed that question: "Who knows. (sic) I have no idea."

People who have studied Wallace and investigated him say that Henry Wallace remains a very dangerous individual. "Do I think Wallace can kill again if he has the opportunity?" asked Charisse Coston, criminologist and professor at the University of North Carolina at Charlotte. Her answer: "Yes, I do."

Sheriff McFadden believes that Wallace is responsible for many more murders than just the ones for which he was convicted. "I believe he killed a lot of people, especially while he was in the navy," McFadden said. "I remember him saying, 'If you take me off Death Row, I can tell you more.' It could be a ploy, but I think he believes he can still play the cat and mouse game with law enforcement."

Whether he can or not, Wallace will remain behind bars, never to see the light of day.

BAD HENRY

Chronology

November 4, 1965 Henry Louis Wallace was born in Barnwell, South Carolina.

Wallace grew up with his mother working long hours as a textile worker.

She was a harsh disciplinarian, constantly criticizing her son for even the smallest mistakes.

Attended Barnwell High School, where he was elected to student council and was a cheerleader.

After he graduated in 1983, Wallace became a disc jockey for a Barnwell radio station.

Wallace went to several colleges before joining the U.S. Navy in 1985.

He married his high school sweetheart, Maretta Brabham, in 1985.

Wallace was honorably discharged from the Navy.

During his time in the Navy, he began using several drugs, including crack cocaine.

In Washington, he was served warrants for several burglaries in and around the Seattle metro area.

In January 1988, Wallace was arrested for breaking into a hardware store. That June, he pled guilty to second-degree burglary. A judge sentenced him to two years of supervised probation.

According to Probation Officer Patrick Seaburg, Wallace did not show up for most mandatory meetings.

On March 8, 1990, he murdered 18-year-old Tashanda Bethea, a Barnwell High School student. He was questioned by the police regarding her disappearance and death, but was never formally charged in her murder.

He was also questioned in connection with the attempted rape of a 16-year-old Barnwell girl, but was never charged for that either.

By that time, his marriage to Maretta had fallen apart. He was fired from his job as Chemical Operator for Sandoz Chemical Co.

In February 1991, he broke into Barnwell High School and the radio station where he once worked as a disc jockey. He stole valuable video and recording equipment and was caught trying to pawn them.

In November 1991, he relocated to Charlotte, North Carolina. He found jobs at several fast-food restaurants in East Charlotte before becoming a manager at Taco Bell near the now-defunct Eastland Mall.

In May 1992, he picked up 33-year-old Sharon Nance, a convicted drug dealer and alleged prostitute. When she demanded payment for her services, Wallace beat her to death, then dropped her body by the railroad tracks. She was found a few days later.

In June 1992, he raped and strangled Caroline Love, 20, at her apartment, then dumped her body in a wooded area. Love was a friend of Wallace's girlfriend.

After he killed Caroline Love, he, his girlfriend, and her sister filed a missing person's report at the police station. It would be almost two years (March 1994) before her body was discovered in a wooded area in Charlotte.

On February 19, 1993, Wallace strangled 20-year-old Shawna Hawk at her home after first raping her and later went to her funeral. Hawk worked at Taco Bell where Wallace was her supervisor.

In March 1993, Hawk's mother, Dee Sumpter, and her godmother, Judy Williams, founded Mothers of Murdered Offspring, a Charlotte-based support group for parents of murdered children.

On June 22, 1993, Wallace raped and strangled his Taco Bell co-worker and manager Audrey Spain, 24. Her body was found two-and-a-half days later on June 25.

On August 10, 1993, Wallace raped and strangled Valencia M. Jumper, a 21-year-old college student from Columbia, S.C. who was a friend of his sister's—then set her on fire to cover up his crime.

A few days after Valencia Jumper's murder, he and his sister went to Valencia's funeral, even sending her family condolences.

A month later, on the night of September 14, 1993, he went to the apartment of 20-year-old Michelle Stinson, a college student and a dedicated single mother of two young sons, aged one and three years old. Stinson was a friend of his from Taco Bell. He raped her and then sometime later strangled and stabbed her in front of her oldest son.

In October 1993, his only child was born.

On February 4, 1994, Wallace was arrested for shoplifting, but police had not made a connection between him and the murders.

On February 20, 1994, a day after Shawna's mother made an appeal to the public to find her daughter's murderer, Wallace raped and strangled Vanessa Little Mack, 25, in her West Charlotte apartment.

On March 8, 1994, Wallace robbed, raped, and strangled 24-year-old Betty Jean Baucom a day after her birthday. Baucom and Wallace's girlfriend were co-workers at Bojangles where she was the assistant manager.

After he murdered Baucom, he took a considerable amount of valuables from the house, then left the apartment with her car. He pawned everything except the car, which he left at a local shopping center across the street from the Lake Apartments.

Wallace went back to the same apartment complex on the night of March 8, 1994, knowing that Verness Woods would be at work so he could murder his girlfriend, Brandi June Henderson.

The police increased their patrols in East Charlotte after two bodies of young Black women were found at The Lake apartment complex.

Even so, Wallace sneaked through to rob and strangle Deborah Ann Slaughter, who had been a co-worker of his girlfriend, and stabbed her some 38 times in the stomach and chest. Her body was found on March 12, 1994.

Wallace was arrested on March 13, 1994. For 12 hours, he confessed to the murders of 10 women in Charlotte. He then confessed to an 11th murder he committed before moving to Charlotte. He described in detail the women's appearances, how he raped, robbed, and killed the women, and his crack habit.

Charlotte's police chief announced Wallace's arrest, reassuring the community that the women of East Charlotte were safe. However, many in the area's Black community criticized the police's conduct during the investigation, accusing them of neglecting the murders of Black women. One woman stated that the police did not care because they viewed the young female murder victims as "fast girls who hang out a lot."

Charlotte's police chief, Dennis Nowicki, had said he was not aware of a killer until early March 1994, when three young Black women were murdered within four days of each other. Charlotte-Mecklenburg Police Department apologized to its residents for not spotting a link among the murders sooner. However, they said the murder cases varied enough to throw them off Wallace's trail. Until Wallace's murder pace picked up in the early weeks of March 1994, the deaths were sporadic and not entirely similar.

It was only in the week of March 9, 1994 that Charlotte Police warned the people in East Charlotte that there was a serial killer on the loose.

Over the next two years, Wallace's trial was delayed over choice of venue, DNA evidence from murdered victims, and jury selection.

His trial began in September 1996. In the opening arguments, prosecutor Marsha Goodenow argued for the death penalty, while defense attorney Isabel Day asked for a life sentence, arguing that Wallace suffered from mental illness, and that the killings were not first-degree murder because they did not result from "premeditation and deliberation."

In 1994, police had asked the FBI for assistance, but the FBI said that the murders were not the work of a serial killer.

Psychologist Faye Sultan testified during the trial that Wallace was a constant victim of physical and mental abuse from his mother since birth and that he suffered from mental illness at the time of the killings. Sultan argued for a life sentence without parole instead of the death penalty.

On January 7, 1997, Wallace was found guilty of nine murders.

On January 29, he was sentenced to nine death sentences.

Following his sentencing, Wallace made a statement to his victims' families, "None of these women, none of your daughters, mothers, sisters (sic) or family members in any way deserved what they got. They did nothing to me that warranted their death."

On June 5, 1998, Wallace married a former prison nurse, Rebecca Torrijas, in a ceremony next to the execution chamber where he has been sentenced to die. Mecklenburg County public defender Isabel Day served as an official witness and photographer. Also attending was the manager of the Death Row unit at the prison.

Since being sentenced to death in 1997, Wallace has been appealing to the courts to overturn the death sentences, stating that his confessions were coerced and his constitutional rights were violated in the process.

The North Carolina Supreme Court upheld the death sentences in 2000.

The U.S. Supreme Court in 2001 denied his appeal.

In 2005, Superior Court Judge Charles Lamm rejected Wallace's latest appeal to overturn his convictions and nine death sentences.

As of March 2023, Henry Louis Wallace was still on North Carolina's death row awaiting execution.

PHOTOS

Henry Wallace As A Young Boy

Henry Wallace, Serial Killer

*Tashanda Bethea, Found Dead In A
Barnwell, South Carolina Pond*

Caroline Love, Wallace's Second Victim In Charlotte

Shawna Hawk, Wallace's Third Victim In Charlotte

Valencia Jumper

Wallace's Fifth Victim In Charlotte

Debra Anne Slaughter, Wallace's Last Victim In Charlotte

*Garry Mcfadden Lead Charlotte
Investigation Of Henry Wallace*

Dee Sumpter, Mother Of Victim Shawna Hawk

ACKNOWLEDGEMENTS

The following people were helpful in the writing of this book. Some of these people were interviewed. Others were helpful with sources and finding or proving information. They are presented in alphabetical order:

Margery Spain Brooks
Ed Carroll
Charisse Coston
Glenn Counts
Lisa Crawford
Eugene 'Buddy" Darnell
Ouida Swan Dest
Tom Hanchett
Stephen Griffith
Darrell Kirkpatrick
Garry McFadden
Linda Moore
Walter Mack
Sonnia Mickle
James Stanberry
Dee Sumpter

The Charlotte Mecklenburg Police Department answered my public record request. The Criminal Department of the Mecklenburg County Clerk of Superior Court provided access to court records. The staffs of York County Public

Library and Winthrop University library in Rock Hill helped with interlibrary loan research requests.

Chief Deputy Rodney M. Collins of the Mecklenburg County Sheriff's Office was helpful in arranging the interview with Sheriff Garry McFadden.

Thanks to my nephew, Pacho Aranda Alvarez, for helping with the photo research and for reading the manuscript.

Thanks to Barbara Casey for editing the manuscript and for her support of my writing career. Much appreciated. Thanks also to Alan Geik for reading the manuscript and offering valuable suggestions.

A special thanks to Dee Sumpter for helping me to get started with the book, for her patience and help in locating sources, and for patiently answering my questions about the Wallace case. I believe I picked up a friend along the way.

I faced one obstacle in writing this book. The crime happened more than three decades ago and some of the sources had died. Some did not want to talk about the Wallace case. I respected their wishes.

SELECTED BIBLIOGRAPHY

A) Books

Burgess, Ann, and Steven Matthew Constantine, *A Killer by Design: Murderers, Mindhunters, and My Quest to Decipher the Criminal Mind*, Hachette Book Group, New York, NY, 2021.

Graves, William, and Heather A. Smith, Charlotte, NC: *The Global Evolution of a New South City*, University of Georgia Press, Athens, GA, 2010.

Grundy, Pamela, *Legacy: Three Centuries of Black History*, Nerve Media Productions LLC, Charlotte, NC, 2022.

Pickens, Cathy, *Charlotte True Crime Stories*. The History Press, Charleston, SC, 2019.

B) Newspapers, Magazines and Wire Services
Associated Press
Charlotte Magazine
New York Times
The Atlantic Magazine
The Howard Journal of Crime and Justice
The People-Sentinel
The State
USA Today
Washington Post

C) Primary

Albarus, Carmeta V., Psychological Study, Henry Wallace, CVA Consulting Services, 1996.

Geringer, Joseph, "Henry Louis Wallace: A Calamity Waiting to Happen," Crime Library, 2011.

Henry Louis Wallace Interview transcripts, 10 hours, Charlotte Metropolitan Police Department, March 12, 1994.

"State of North Carolina v Henry Louis Wallace," Supreme Court of North Carolina, No. 241A97, Decided May 5, 2000.

Supplemental Reports, Charlotte Police Department, 1993-94.

Wallace v Polk, Opinion, 3:05cv464-C, May 5, 2008.

D) Internet sources

Coston Charisse and Joseph Kuhns, *Lives Interrupted: A Case Study of Henry Louis Wallace—an African American Serial murderer in a Rapidly Expanding Southern City*, The Department of Criminal Justice, UNCC, Charlotte, North Carolina.

Episode 49:*Henry Louis Wallace: The Taco Bell Strangler* https://www.youtube.com/watch?v=6lSnNVs-548.

Episode 166: *Serial Killer: Henry Louis Wallace* https://www.youtube.com/watch?v=sbl7EyHnm5E, https://www.youtube.com/watch?v=43reU3BlMzI.

First Blood https://www.youtube.com/watch?v=CbNRdWJIOcg.

He was a Menace!!! Serial Killer: "Bad Henry" Louis Wallace (The Taco Bell Killer).

Henry Louis Wallace https://www.youtube.com/watch?v=2bYjyxjokr8.

Henry Louis Wallace https://www.youtube.com/watch?v=ijYseZldtTs.

Henry Louis Wallace: Serial killer https://www.youtube.com/watch?v=HSruZjDjlWs.

Henry Louis Wallace, The Taco Bell Strangler by Reigning Blood https://www.youtube.com/watch?v=xiDLZxzRRRQ.

I am Homicide, TV series, Investigative Discovery, 2016 https://www.investigationdiscovery.com/show/i-am-homicide-investigation-discovery.

SE5 EP235 *Feels like Henry Louis Wallace Could've Been Stopped* https://www.youtube.com/watch?v=7PHPLSK3VNw.

Serial Killer: "Bad Henry" Louis Wallace (The Taco Bell Killer) https://www.youtube.com/watch?v=pr-qP0n4qNE.

The Taco Bell Strangler https://www.youtube.com/watch?v=O4_1MpwB1mc.

The Taco Bell Strangler | Henry Louis Wallace and Victims https://www.youtube.com/watch?v=lpcVtxh5Ojg

ABOUT THE AUTHOR

Ron Chepesiuk is an optioned screenwriter, documentary producer, and the award-winning author of more than 40 books. He is a former professor and head of the Archives at Winthrop University in South Carolina. He is a two-time Fulbright Scholar to Indonesia and Bangladesh and a former instructor in UCLA Extension's Journalism Department.

His articles, which number in the thousands, have appeared in such publications as *FHM, USA Today, Black Enterprise, Woman's World, Modern Maturity, New York Times Syndicate, Toronto Star, Los Angeles Times Syndicate, Bulletin of Atomic Scientists,* among others. His documentary on Frank Matthews, legendary drug kingpin, which he produced and directed, won the Silver Doc award at the Las Vegas International Film Festival. Four of his screenplays are currently in development for feature movies and four of his books have been optioned for movies. His script, *Death Fences,* was the grand winner of the Amsterdam, Holland-based 2019 New Visions International Film Festival.

As an expert in crime history, he is a consultant to the Gangland TV series and has been interviewed on numerous TV networks and programs, including Discovery, NBC Dateline, History, Biography, ID, Reelz, Black Entertainment Television, Starz, and TV 1. As a journalist, Ron has reported from more than thirty-five countries, including Cuba, Northern Ireland, Colombia, Kenya, Hong Kong, and Nepal, and his 16,000 plus interviews include such luminaries as Gerry Adams, Yasser Arafat, John Kerry, Evander Holyfield, Jimmy Carter, Andy McDow, Abbie Hoffman, a former president of Nicaragua, and three former presidents and two vice presidents of Colombia, South America.

Ron is also radio host of CRIME BEAT Radio Show. The Crime Beat show has been on the air since January 2011 and has listeners in 160 plus countries. Guests have included Robert Kennedy, Jr., Henry Hill, Noam Chomsky, George Jung, Joe Piston (aka Donnie Brasco), F. Lee Bailey, and Chris Kyle, American sniper.

For More News About Ron Chepesiuk,
Signup For Our Newsletter:

http://wbp.bz/newsletter

Word-of-mouth is critical to an author's long-term success. If you appreciated this book please leave a review on the Amazon sales page:

http://wbp.bz/badhenry

Index

ALSO FROM RON CHEPESIUK

THE REAL MR BIG
http://wbp.bz/realmrbiga

HOT NEW RELEASES

DEATH BY TALONS
http://wbp.bz/deathbytalons

LOU AND JONBENÉT

A Legendary Lawman's Quest To Solve
A Child Beauty Queen's Murder

John Wesley Anderson

LOU & JONBENET
http://wbp.bz/louandjonbenet

BY THE HOST OF *TRUE CRIME GARAGE*

NIC EDWARDS

WITH BRIAN WHITNEY

THE DELPHI MURDERS
http://wbp.bz/delphi

www.ingramcontent.com/pod-product-compliance
Lightning Source LLC
Chambersburg PA
CBHW061152120626
46546CB00005B/2029